MANIPULISM AND THE WEAPON OF GUILT

COLLECTIVISM EXPOSED

BY MIKKEL CLAIR NISSEN

Original layout by Sea Hill Press Inc.
http://www.seahillpress.com
Santa Barbara, California

Published by
CDES Publishing LLC, Las Vegas, Nevada
http://www.cdespublishing.com

Manipulism and the Weapon of Guilt
Collectivism Exposed
Library of Congress Control Number: 2015939944
ISBN 13: 978-1-63396-025-1
ISBN 10: 1633960250

Printed in the United States of America

NOTES

Manipulism and the Weapon of Guilt: Collectivism Exposed is the utmost controversial exposé and carefully detailed description of the awful emotional mind game that facilitates communism, socialism, fascism, and social-liberalism, known as collectivism. The book exposes Denmark, the supposed happiest nation on earth, for what it truly is: collectivism's biggest propaganda hoax. Danish author Mikkel Clair Nissen tells the hidden facts and realities of life in Denmark's democratic socialism that they never want you to know.

Disclaimer

Mikkel Clair Nissen does not hold a degree in any form of psychotherapy, but he has dedicated over a decade to psychopathology, specializing in narcissistic personality disorder (NPD). The contents of this book are not meant to substitute for professional help or counseling. Hence, the reader is encouraged to use the material for both internal as well as external observations. Diagnoses and treatment of personality disorders should only be carried out by specially trained professionals.

Table Of Contents

INTRODUCTION

The most illusive notion known to the modern age is that altruistic egalitarian ideals of the left-wing—known as Marxism—are perceived as ideologies. Social-liberalism, which is the first step toward socialism with the intent to achieve communism, merely defines the severity of inferiority complex: the extremely tiny gap between pathological narcissism and its more extreme form known as narcissistic personality disorder (NPD).

Growing up in a collective society, one is coerced, and virtually left with all but one choice. As a former socialist, finally liberated, who was born and raised in Denmark—supposedly the happiest nation on earth—I have devoted my life to alerting the world about the subliminal secrets of collectivism. How can anyone truly fight anything if one is not 100 percent aware and able to describe exactly what one is fighting?

My intention in this book is to prove that one single voice, with the right words, can have the roar of a million and can influence the world by creating a precise understanding of democratic socialism—or to be more precise and use the latest terminology, "universal welfare society." Thus, the more appropriate terminology to describe Marxism's democratic passive-aggressive approach—rather than the usual obvious and complete fascist military takeover—would be "ambient socialism." Thereby, simply with the weapon of irrefutable knowledge, Marxism can be immobilized. Quite simply, exposure will cause sudden awareness, and socialism, democratically, is less likely achieved once its awful emotional mind game has become common household knowledge. This book, therefore, is dedicated to freedom and the earth's greatest individualistic culture, the United States of America.

This exposure, based almost entirely on social science, is so controversial and comprehensively detailed that Denmark's perceived right-wing newspaper—ironically the same newspaper that caused the Muhammad cartoons controversy in 2005 in the name of freedom of speech—will not review my book. This explicative psychological index (e.g., collectivist traits, indoctrination methods, intimidation techniques, and ways of passive coercion) is meant as a gift from me to the reader for self-empowerment through social observations, as well as a subconscious journey for the readers themselves. Please share this knowledge with friends and support my effort to alert the world.

The intimidations (threats, lies, and deceptions) in attempt to discredit me and deny this book's honesty and preciseness are all worth my while. Regardless, this book will raise questions and effect societal changes, and the outcome will speak for itself. Wars should be fought with words—the right words—and never through coercion or terror. Welcome to my words of revolution.

"The world will not be destroyed by those who do evil, but by those who watch them without doing anything."
—ALBERT EINSTEIN

CHAPTER ONE

WAKING UP ON THE DARK SIDE OF THE OBVIOUS TRUTH

For several years I have felt obligated to tell my side of this story, especially since the climate convention COP15 in Copenhagen in December 2009, where Oprah Winfrey visited Denmark and later proclaimed that Danes were the happiest people in the world. She was supported by data from Dr. Adrian White, PhD in sociology from the British University of Leicester. Ironically, for over five decades—in the era 1950–2006—Denmark's suicide rate has averaged just about double that of the United States. Also, Denmark has a much higher rate of alcohol consumption. Moreover, in the same five decades, Denmark's suicide rate has averaged almost triple that of the United Kingdom, countries with the exact same climates. In addition, Denmark has one of the world's highest consumption rates of antidepressant medications, a rate that is steadily on the rise. Undeniably, Denmark's suicide rate has been reduced to a more moderate rate. These statistics are nonetheless deeply misleading since excessive usage of suppressant medications in Denmark are responsible for subordinating, in addition to obscuring, what would otherwise be a much higher suicide rate. Something here simply does not add up, making it difficult for me to agree with Oprah. Unfortunately, all countries have a darker side of the obvious truth.

Not much longer than a decade ago, the way I thought and acted was absolutely no different than the thoughts and actions of any of my fellow citizens. I acted impulsively and subconsciously, indoctrinated with my country's oppressive inhibitive mentality. My intellectual transformation took place slowly, after having traveled and worked for many years abroad.

In the same way that a religious person might spread the news, I proudly promoted Denmark's collective way of thinking by telling everyone the story about the great and wonderful country named Denmark and bragging equally as much about how great it was to be a Dane.

I slowly began to compare the reality I grew up in to the reality I encountered in the United States, Australia, and Spain. This comparison brought me to see a completely different truth about my own country. It was a reality that few Danes had seen before then. After living a life as a socialist and absolute nationalist who promoted my country as open and caring, I now felt totally deceived when confronted with the reality. I felt embarrassed by the fact that I had personally traveled the world for so many years promoting socialism and a nation that was, and still is, absolutely contrary to what I claimed. Indeed, Denmark is a deprived society living in absolute denial.

Though I despise living here, Denmark is to some extent a bearable place to live, but it is far from better than other nations and not any more socially happy. Danes are best known for being some of the coldest and most reserved people in the world, with neurotic behavior resulting from oppressive, collectivist mentality.

I had a poor yet reasonably decent childhood in Denmark's then safer society. I grew up among socialists in Denmark's democratic socialism and was indoctrinated by family, friends, and fellow citizens, and consequently I was assimilated into their vicious, oppressive pathological mind game.

I once told a friend that I felt like the Danes owned my thoughts through their continuous attempt to undermine my true individual self. He replied, "Maybe they should pay rent then." Though I thought this a cute remark, as an entrepreneur who has risen from the lowest parts of society and achieved an independent lifestyle, I constantly have to be on guard not to trigger my fellow citizens' inferior, inhibitive emotions. In Denmark, unlike in the United States, it is important to avoid social-status confrontations, and instead to give way to the ordinary denigration and envy—the extreme inferiority complex facilitating democratic socialism—though my self-imposed consciousness tells me that I most definitely have the right to be proud of my achievements and shout them out loud.

It was not until I went abroad at the age of nineteen that I started waking up. It was a journey that did not end until fourteen years later. In this period, I spent numerous summer seasons in Spain working in such jobs as bouncer, club management, and club marketing. I lived several years in the United States, the country that taught me to see, and eventually liberated me from Marxism's strong mental iron grip. For a deeply brainwashed socialist, coerced from childhood to resent the American lifestyle, coming to the United States was the culture shock of a lifetime. My eyes were opened to the undermining measures that Danish society had placed upon me and the realization that this undermining was the prime determiner of my level of self-worth. My lack of self-esteem resulted in a subconscious war between will and vanity that later turned out to be a mental safeguard against any insight into liberty.

First impressions easily mislead, as in the case of Oprah's view of Denmark. One neither sees a person's true character nor a country's true nature until having become truly familiarized. Likewise, one must leave one's natural societal surroundings to truly see and understand its hidden side. This personal story, this exposure, is the exact reason why totalitarian-collective societies (e.g., China, North Korea, and Cuba) restrict information and the right to travel.

I slowly began to compare the enormous differences I observed on my journeys, not only between cultures but also in regard to mentality and behavior. Upon every return to Denmark, I gradually became more and more aware that something was awfully wrong with my country. Like a dysfunctional family, Danes are familiarized all through life with their particular behaviors; thus, they think it is seemingly normal to live with these dysfunctions. Danes, regardless of social status, are terribly insecure. They are always picked on, compulsively corrected and policed, and regularly intimidated by each other. Known in psychology as pathological narcissism, these behaviors are a way of everyday life.

Danes are distant, unlike Americans, whose confident mentality is friendly, uplifting, open, and encouraging. Foreigners often have the impression—due to feelings of inferiority—that Americans are too confident.

Truly baffling were the differences between the unprivileged people in Denmark and those of the United States. The unprivileged people are unmotivated, miserable, and neurotic in my own country, though the government (the taxpayer) spoils them with everything. America's monetary lower class, who are given little or nothing by the government, are still ambitious, open, curious, and confident—in pursuit of happiness—regardless of their social or economic class.

Truly mystifying was the fact that Americans, living in a nation with a great deal higher crime level than Denmark's, are less apprehensive by far. In the beginning, I simply thought that the United States was culturally different. Then I met and fell in love with an Australian girl, and eventually I moved to Australia. In Australia, I realized how far from the truth I had been.

I felt puzzled by the apparent link between oppressive collective-societal norms—more specifically Scandinavia's most famous expression, "Don't think that you are more than others!"—and socialism, with its intent to socially equilibrate. There was evidently more to Marxism's norms than meets the eye. "Who else but the envious, inferior mind would have the need to debase others?"

Rather opposite to what I was used to, it quite simply became obvious that self-encouragement and self-assurance not only were positive but also were actually appreciated, encouraged, and valued in liberated cultures, where the individual is expected to claim responsibility for oneself. My whole life I had been indoctrinated to think that Scandinavian mentality was normal, and in addition I had been persuaded to believe it was truly unique. Yet in my work, first in Spain with East-Europeans—people from behind the former communist Iron Curtain—and then in Australia, a country located thousands of miles away from my own, the patterns of inferior behavioral, narcissistic similarities were overwhelming. Although still a conservative but largely Marxist-influenced society, Australia was not yet a truly democratic socialist nation. Australia was, however, clearly in the ambient transition and final stages of radicalization when I lived there. There I met the exact same ignorantly arrogant resentment toward Americans. Australians used the same comments and phrases as the Danes, had the exact same suppressed, condemning mentality, and even had a name for this mentality: the tall poppy syndrome. This was my wake-up call. I slowly developed an interest in political ideologies, behavioral science, and psychopathology, and eventually I developed an interest in the social-psychological impact that different ideologies have on personal psyche, identity, and mentality. Thereby, I began connecting the pieces in a mind-breaking sociological and psychological puzzle.

AN EVERYDAY STORY

In 2009, I attended a course on sports science. On a break while attending class, some students and I were sitting outside enjoying the sunshine of the last days of summer. I remember one of the girls started to explain that her boyfriend had invited her to accompany him on a holiday to the United States. And with what slowly became an arrogant attitude, she now explained, "I have never been there and will never go. Americans are stupid and arrogant, and they don't care about anyone!" I instantly felt compelled to intervene, and I replied, "I disagree. I have lived in the United States, and I think Americans are absolutely beautiful people. Curious that you just used the word 'arrogant' as you have just explained that you have never been to the United States. So how can you know with certainty that Americans are stupid and arrogant?" I further explained, "Trust me! We Danes are no better than any of the Americans I have ever met, and I personally remember a fun story about a Danish woman at a Manhattan mall who purposely left her stroller unattended outside on a street in the middle of New York with her infant child in it. She was arrested for doing this; thereafter, her husband quite quickly divorced her. So maybe you should mow your own lawn before you do it next door?" The girl never got to make a reply. Instead, one of the other male students instantly stood up and shouted at me, "Maybe you should move to America then!" He quickly left.

NOTE: Do not fool yourself, as this entire book's everyday examples are typical everyday experiences performed by seemingly ordinary, well-educated, and upstanding people. Bringing me to the point that, because of this suppressive collectivist mentality, when confronted with self-identifiable truths or reverse criticism—in fact any disapproval—Danes absolutely lack the ability to take any criticism; therefore, they generally fail to confer before the conversation or debate has even started.

I know I can be awfully sharp and direct, as I do not put up with ignorant arrogance and two-facedness. Bear in mind that I was born in Denmark, and my Danish family tree dates back hundreds of years. Although I have neither signed any contract nor chosen to be born here, my own fellow countrymen evidently feel they are more entitled to reside here than I am, as they are clearly ready to go so low as to ask me to leave my own country just because I utter my opinion with even the least criticism.

Our radicalized, socialistically influenced consciousness has created a supposedly wonderful and caring utopian society that takes care of almost everyone. One unfortunate aspect of democratic socialism is that the family's obligation to parent the children has been completely disabled and replaced with Big Mother Denmark, the government. This new collectivism has essentially immobilized the individual effort of parenting, and Big Mother Denmark nourishes the Danes from birth until death. Life is designed completely without any kind of consequence. Of course, this is true only until one opposes the system or authorities. The apathetic government is ready to sacrifice any integrity to achieve its desired result, and the outcome is a non-defiant, passive, and absolutely conformist authoritarian nation. Apart from still seemingly possessing the right to freedom of speech, as well as supposedly living in a democracy, Denmark is only minutely different from the former Soviet Union or East Germany. What the master commands, the puppet does. Citizens of Denmark never question anything, unless of course an entitlement benefit is to be taken away.

I recall the time when my daughter had to have a vaccine injection at the age of five. Like many other parents, I told her a few days beforehand. I told her that it would hurt a little, but only for a moment. Yet when it was over, she would get the biggest ice cream available. This is exactly how collectivism blinds the frail mind. The only thing my daughter would think about was the ice cream, not the pain.

This seemingly democratic country is a bureaucracy with laws, rules, and regulations for absolutely everything. Yet, there is no actual justice or punishment for breaking them. Sentencing citizens based on assumptions and circumstantial evidence is, however, ordinary. The accused is guilty until proven innocent. The society is set up to ensure that the populace can intimidate (police) one another. And while Americans debate gun policies, Danes are not even at liberty to own pepper spray. Neither are we at liberty to protect ourselves or the privacy of our homes. This is any criminal's haven, with such lack of consequence that one could literally kill numerous people intentionally and still die an unincarcerated citizen.

While in this nanny nation, where everything is served on a silver platter, the question is not whether one needs to work, but if one actually cares to work. Artificial impregnation, free of personal charge to people who obviously cannot afford a child in the first place, has slowly sneaked its way onto the menu of almost unlimited pity benefits, right along with breast implants and holidays. No doubt, to some this would sound ideal. Yet in reality, it is quite the contrary.

Democracy in itself cannot radicalize collectivism. Therefore, socialism within the context of a democratic system is very different from traditional socialism. In an attempt to protect, maintain, and secure the continuance of what has now ended up in absolute collectivist greed, the Marxists have put into use awful methods of suppressive psychological undermining. Now we find they use orchestrated, designed, and calculated psychological coercion—subliminal conditioning that utilizes the weapon of guilt and enticement. Coercion is accomplished by means that are identical to the methods commonly known as Machiavellian egocentricity, which is described in psychology as the illusive ability to manipulate, subdue, and control others in order to achieve personal ends and desires. This results in weakening the general society, and even worse, further weakening society's emotionally weakest citizens—the co-dependent collectivists. Conversely, this emotional weakness empowers the radical collectivist part of society even further. The more deprived the collectivist is—and thereby the more manipulative and malignant—the stronger the collectivist.

NOTE: The political spectrum, known as right and left, is in actuality being purposely manipulated. The fact is that the essence of freedom lies in the proper limitation of government. Indisputably, throughout history no source has proven itself more deadly and destructive than the authority invested in government. While this is general knowledge to those who enthusiastically advocate freedoms, most, unfortunately, are uninformed. Accordingly, this creates the perfect environment for deception. Indeed, an accurate political spectrum from right to left would undeniably begin with "freedom" (e.g., non-intrusive government, self-sovereignty, and self-determination), defined by "little or no government control." Thus, the political spectrum would end up on the left with "totalitarianism" (e.g., authoritarian dictatorial government, subjugation, and tyranny), defined by "unlimited government control." In accordance, a correct paradigm would begin with ideals of "anarchy," endorsing "no government." Next would come the ideals of "libertarianism," also known as "classical-liberalism," endorsing "limited government." Thereafter, would come "modern-liberalism," also known as "social-liberalism," endorsing "greater government." Ultimately, the spectrum would end with the ideals of "fascism," "socialism," and "communism," endorsing "totalitarian government."

Conversely, perfect deception is achieved through manipulating this spectrum by placing those who are in favor of egalitarianism (the notion of social equality), also known as Marxism (e.g., communists and socialists), on the left wing. This would place those who are not in favor of social equality on the right wing, which is more than half of the political spectrum, including fascists who are in favor of complete government control. Although the fact is that communism, socialism, and fascism promote the same set of radical collectivist ideals of "totalitarianism"—dictatorial intrusive government. However, by affiliating genuine right-wingers—individuals in favor of minimum government control—with totalitarian fascist regimes (e.g., Hitler's "Nazism"), the perfect diversion is created.

Hence, relying on ignorance, the left and right paradigm is in fact a well-known method of deception, known as "divide and conquer," with one sole purpose: to create confusion and so achieve emotional and intellectual control.

This technique consequently sets up the populace against one another, while allowing those who want to remain in authority to promote and achieve their exact agenda, "totalitarianism"—total government control.

Although, I am not particularly in favor of the left versus right paradigm, essentially believing these to be but variations and severities of a similar set of problems, known as conformism. Thus, it is necessary that I utilize the paradigm as doing so allows me to further exemplify how this perfect deception is employed.

Accordingly, nations in Europe are generally so far left wing—perfectly fueled by the deceptive left and right paradigm—that the left-wing "social liberal," more commonly known in the United States simply as the "liberal" or "modern liberal" is perceived to be ultra-right wing and often even considered by European left wingers to be right-wing extremists. However, caused and controlled by the endlessly immense left-wing subliminal suppression in Europe, my research shows that the American liberal and the European social liberal are generally in no way emotionally compatible. America still has a chance to turn its great nation in the right direction.

As a Dane who was born and raised in Denmark, I will, through my personal knowledge of my country, my culture, and its citizens, carefully take the reader step by step through ten years of extensive social-psychological research and observations to show that Denmark is collectivism's biggest propaganda hoax. I further intend to prove that Danes—virtually all authoritarian government supporters (communists, socialists, fascists, and social liberals)—are being subjugated, unlike genuine freedom enthusiasts. I will prove that the happiest people on earth, supposedly the Danes, do not have any option to create their happiness, but only to imagine being happy.

Furthermore, this book will carefully teach the reader how a democratically, socialistic-infiltrated government, in this case Denmark's, is completely controlled. It is dominated entirely by only a minority of society's absolute weakest citizens through an emotional process that disables and mentally enslaves the majority of society. The result is the exact in nature to the Stockholm syndrome.

Creating falsified contentment (learned helplessness)—through entitlement benefits combined with suppressive manipulation, emotional coercion, and reverse psychology—results in feelings of inferiority and co-dependency, thereby achieving the perfect societal mind control: manipulism.

I will further teach how my former political viewpoints work sociologically and psychologically, and I will prove that the key that facilitates collectivism is severe pathological narcissism. This book will in fact demonstrate that various but severe levels of deprived mental health drive a majority of Marxists: the mental illness of narcissistic personality disorder (NPD). These supposed ideologies are all founded and facilitated by one single source: malignant narcissistic coercion. By means of destroying true individualism and mental freedom, and emotionally weakening its citizens, Denmark has necessitated co-dependency and attained its goal of accomplishing the perfect human organism for the intent of fabricating social equilibrium. Ultimately, these methods create perfectly subjugated human beings, insecure people who are, or will be, at an absolute standstill through most of their lives. These are people who cannot take criticism or respond rationally to any criticism—people who are more or less disabled from questioning or criticizing their political views, the government, or their country. This is all the result of perfect coercive collectivist mind control with an iron grip so powerful that it reaches the farthest right-wing political parties of society, radicalizing otherwise right-wing individualistic politics. In other words, this book will explain how Denmark accomplished the creation of the world's most seemingly free society, which is actually the "perfect" totalitarian state—a society completely without a political right wing. This is the ultimate goal of democratic socialism, or what I choose to refer to as neo-communism.

The following disclosure is absolutely not unique to Denmark. This book only uses Denmark as an example, although no country in the world could ever serve as a better example. While Denmark and other similar Scandinavian societies are exceptional and quite unlike anywhere else, this path is in various degrees identical for all countries in the newly monopolized, democratic-socialism superstate known as the European Union. In fact, this process is taking place to some degree all over the world, and now the process has come to take its turn in the United States.

The monetary part is the least of Marxism's problems. If it were not for what this book is essentially about, my growing awareness and exposing of collectivism's awful subliminal secrets, I would definitely be a socialist today. Generosity does not come from collectivism—it comes from the heart!

If anything slightly positive can be said about Marxism, it is that Scandinavia's democratic socialism is history's closest attempt toward accomplishing the impossible. Yet, it has been accomplished only because Denmark is a small society with a population of a mere 5.5 million, and it has occurred through absolute mental coercion, propaganda, secrecy, and denial. A society undermined by a perceived ideology that in its humanitarian, pathological make-believe attempt of caring for society's weakest, literally creates them. The wall to the former communist Iron Curtain might have fallen visually, but the building of the intellectual wall still proceeds. The wall never fell; it opened.

In reality, the democratic process, merely balanced by the center-left–wing social liberals, is the only remaining measure keeping the socialist, communist, and fascist part of society from initiating their true tyrannical agenda. Socialism, communism, fascism, and social liberalism—known as collectivism—are not ideologies, but severities of pathological narcissism—magical thinking of infinite excuses.

"The perfect totalitarian state is one where the all-powerful political bosses and their army of managers control a population of slaves who do not have to be coerced because they love their servitude."

—PAT BUCHANAN

CHAPTER TWO
COLD WAR II

Collectivists will read this book, but in an attempt to deny the evidence, they will not really read it thoroughly. Instead, they subconsciously will look for ways to distract themselves from the facts. Any excuse is valid. If it is not looking for spelling mistakes, then it will be looking for research errors. Then they would want to see proof of a PhD, yet even a PhD would not be enough. Unless of course one uses the PhD to establish how happy Danes are. A collectivist will always deny, belittle, and intimidate, but never truly research. Severe pathological narcissism (more precisely a mindset referred to in psychology as "magical thinking") is the key to collectivism's progression, survival, and continuance.

I once sat admiring my daughter, aged six, doing crazy things interactively with a children's program on TV. At one point she glanced at me, smiled, and said, "Am I not skilled daddy?" "Yes, you are very, very clever," I replied. The situation made me think about the mental freedom that my daughter still possesses. A mental freedom still liberated from my country's oppressive collectivist mentality: the right to be her unique self and confidently express herself freely. She will be deprived of this mental freedom by Marxism's powerful emotional iron grip here in Denmark if I do not teach her how to protect herself from it. This mental prison is an oppressive collectivist mentality that has been misunderstood and misinterpreted through almost a century. It is perceived simply to be Scandinavian culture, described as the Jante Law.

The Jante Law/Subliminal Conditioning (Malignant Narcissistic Coercion)

> **Don't think you are anything special!**
>
> **Don't think you are as good as us!**
>
> **Don't think you are wiser than us!**
>
> **Don't convince yourself that you are better than us!**
>
> **Don't think you know more than us!**
>
> **Don't think you are more important than us!**
>
> **Don't think you are good at anything!**
>
> **Don't laugh at us!**
>
> **Don't think anyone cares about you!**
>
> **Don't think you can teach us anything!**

The Jante Law was first described in the novel *A Fugitive Crosses His Track* in 1933 by the Danish author Axel Sandemose. His observations and thoughts describe the consequence of more or less three-quarters of a century of continuous advancement of oppressive collectivist mentality in the Danish society. The fictional Danish town of Jante lives by its own ten commandments, named the Jante Law. This slow intellectual process of radicalization started roughly a few decades before *The Communist Manifesto* was published in 1848 by the Germans Karl Marx and Friedrich Engels, when the utopian idea of socialism was originally presented in the United States in 1825 by Robert Owen, a Welshman.

The Jante Law is unquestionably not a unique Scandinavian phenomenon. The mentality is commonly known worldwide. In commonwealth countries such as Australia, New Zealand, Canada, and Great Britain, it is referred to as tall poppy syndrome, a pejorative term that is more frequently used in the most socialistic-influenced of these nations. The term is also referred to as schadenfreude (referring to someone envious and scornful who takes pleasure in demeaning others), a loanword used in English from the German word schadenfroh that is commonly used in the democratic socialism countries of Scandinavia (i.e., Denmark, Norway, Sweden, and Finland) as well as in Russia. Behind the former communist Iron Curtain, the mentality is also known as hell (e.g., in Poland as Polish hell). In all cases, these syndromes are uniquely linked to Marxism, the notion of social equality—all forms of fascism. Whether called crab mentality in the Philippines ("If I can't have it neither can you") or the Jante Law in Scandinavia ("Don't think that you are more than others"), the tall poppy syndrome in Marxist-influenced commonwealth countries ("Cutting down the tall poppy"), or schadenfreude in former Nazi-occupied Germany, these syndromes all describe the same condition of pathological narcissism that thrives commonly in collectivism on undermining and is driven by severe inferiority complex. Depending on how severely deprived the person's self-esteem is, the consequent result can be narcissistic personality disorder (NPD).

Narcissistic behaviors occur as defense mechanisms, described as the lack of ability to take criticism as a result of low self-worth or feeling inferior in certain situations. We are all born as narcissists and gradually mature our immature narcissistic ego into a healthy subconscious adult identity. Unhealthy narcissism appears in this stage of development if the process of the emerging individual self is by some means disrupted. Should narcissistic behaviors or feelings reoccur frequently, be strong or tough to control, this is then referred to in psychology as pathological narcissism. Frequently, this is caused by poor standards set by others, such as intervention by parents, friends, and society.

HOTCHKISS' SEVEN DEADLY SINS OF NARCISSISM

Hotchkiss identified what she called the seven deadly sins of narcissism:

Shamelessness: Shame is the feeling that lurks beneath all unhealthy narcissism and the inability to process shame in healthy ways.

Magical thinking: Narcissists see themselves as perfect, using distortion and illusion known as magical thinking. They also use projection to dump shame onto others.

Arrogance: A narcissist who is feeling deflated may re-inflate by diminishing, debasing, or degrading somebody else.

Envy: A narcissist may secure a sense of superiority in the face of another person's ability by using contempt to minimize the other person.

Entitlement: Narcissists hold unreasonable expectations of particularly favorable treatment and automatic compliance because they consider themselves special. Failure to comply is considered an attack on their superiority, and the perpetrator is considered an "awkward" or "difficult" person. Defiance of their will is a narcissistic injury that can trigger narcissistic rage.

Exploitation: Can take many forms but always involves the exploitation of others without regard for their feelings or interests. Often the other is in a subservient position where resistance would be difficult or even impossible. Sometimes the subservience is not so much real as assumed.

Bad boundaries: Narcissists do not recognize that they have boundaries and that others are separate and are not extensions of themselves. Others either exist to meet their needs or may as well not exist at all. Those who provide narcissistic supply to the narcissist are treated as if they are part of the narcissist and are expected to live up to those expectations. In the mind of a narcissist, there is no boundary between self and other.

The narcissist feels emotionally threatened when other individuals appear confident or challenging, creating an urge to belittle, intimidate, or humiliate. This is referred to in psychology as malignant narcissism. These emotions are caused by arrogance and envy, and are triggered by criticism, undesired reality, facts, and insights, or anything that appears superior to the narcissist's "sense of worth," characterized in psychology by "the sense of entitlement." What better place to be for the narcissist: to be worshipped, to be in a superior mind-controlling position (such as psychiatry, tutoring, media, or politics), or to be part of a complete collective society adapted to these coercive, narcissistic societal manners, and the resultant universal pathological narcissism, where everyone expresses themselves as equals.

Though nearly an exact description of oppressive collectivist mentality, Sandemose's novel still has a few inconsistencies. One example is that one is allowed to think greatly of oneself but is intimidated into never expressing it in obvious ways. I have, therefore, carefully clarified the mentality for which basis I elaborate in the following description of the mentality's behavior, that is, though minutely different, the mentality known around the world as tall poppy syndrome.

The tall poppy syndrome, with its origin in Australia, dates back to the 1860s, just after *The Communist Manifesto* was published. It refers to a powerful yet common mentality that people of all countries are subject to in some degree. Symptoms include bullying as a completely normal part of any child's process of building identity and self-esteem. Among adults, contemptuous behavior and malignant narcissism is routinely performed by envious immature people who are driven by severe pathological narcissism and lack initiative, and as a result exploit the easy way by trying to bring down surrounding individuals to their low level of accomplishment. Consequently, depending on a country's level of radical collectivist influence, the mentality—when adopted by collectivists and continued into adulthood—is unequivocally transformed into manipulism.

SOCIAL–PSYCHOLOGICAL THEORY: MANIPULISM

To lower self-esteem, consequently generating feelings of inferiority and co-dependency—subjectively destroying independence; to thereby facilitate complete intellectual control with fictive contentment.

Ideologies are replaceable with an emotional scale, a psychological index by means of only five topics of significance: (1) collectivism (co-dependency) versus individualism (independency); (2) the ability to maintain positive personal boundaries between self and other (e.g., normative egoism) versus the inability or unwillingness to maintain personal boundaries between self and other (egocentrism and narcissism); (3) self-motivation by, and prioritization of, individual self-interests (e.g., normative egoism) versus forcing upon others one's ideals for personal interests (severe pathological narcissism); (4) contentment versus discontentment; and (5) evading personal responsibility versus claiming individual responsibility.

Tall poppy syndrome, belittlement as part of the process of building one's identity, takes place in all nations around the world, especially in the school system among the youth. Almost all of us have been bullied in school or have bullied others. Even in cultures with adults who are largely independent and liberated mentally, all people are collectivists throughout their dependent childhood and teen years. The major difference is that dependency lessens as liberated cultures endorse the emerging individual self through encouraging individuality and independence by way of supporting confident self-encouragement, self-assurance, and benign envy, all of which raise the level of self-esteem. Once dependency decreases, the belittlement wears off with age. Yet in democratic socialism, to accomplish, protect, and maintain social equality and authoritarian dominance, the inferiority complexes and schoolyard bullying gradually intensify into pathological narcissism in the teenage years, and ultimately into manipulism. Inevitably, calculated adult bullying—malignant narcissism—continues all through life.

In the last century, the tall poppy syndrome (though it would best reflect its appalling behavior if it were in fact named "tall puppy" syndrome, in relation to the way a small dog will show its power through loud barking and hostile actions toward larger dogs to whom it feels inferior) has simply been described as bullying, where the weakest, driven by low self-esteem, pick on the strongest. In the case of democratic socialism, instead of the usual one or a few individuals being weakened, the whole citizenry is slowly shaped into an oppressed society. Accordingly, when the frailest parts of society are given a promise of social equality, this sets in motion the syndrome of manipulism through the process of learned helplessness, via government bribery, that weakens them further. The incentive to create vital self-esteem is corrupted; consequently, basic human survival instinct slowly shapes an envious, oppressive organism. In other words, the schoolyard bullying, the usual "madness shared by two"—referred to in psychology as *folie à deux*—is slowly nationalized. The organism, at this point a potent collective unity, again always with its origin in the frailer parts of society and driven by envy, is ready to exploit others for personal gain. All of this is the result of severe pathological narcissism, which stems from feelings of excessive self-importance and magical thinking that generate illusions of extreme moral superiority (unification by fantasies of the perfect utopian society without any poverty, where all people have equal opportunities and are treated entirely equally), justification for excessive entitlement, and expectations of unreasonable, favorable treatment without mandatory achievement. Ignorance, denial, omniscience (magical thinking), and a lack of ability to take criticism further result in arrogance.

Additionally, lack of ambition and the urge to feel equal is the source of envy. To mentally denigrate and socially assimilate becomes its common goal. What takes over is learned helplessness: human nature's basic survival instinct. The mentality is one of personality mind control of malignant narcissistic coercion in an attempt to weaken and disable society's natural source of questioning and criticism. To achieve, protect, and maintain collective accomplishments, the mass mentality is slowly shaped and gradually accepted into all levels of society as common behavior.

This is all a perfectly harmonious process that slowly replaces actual individual contentment with "co-dependency"; referred to in psychology as a dysfunctional relationship where a person—typically the stronger party—becomes psychologically submissive and dependent on pleasing others (e.g., nurturing their addiction, their poor mental health, immaturity, irresponsibility, or under-achievement, or by mimicking other people's opinions in need of continuous relations). Public narcissistic trends increase as society grows weaker, with the initial warnings being excessive entitlement and an increase in traits such as bad boundaries, magical thinking, and failure to accept responsibility for personal actions. In addition, a rise in bullying is evident in the largely radical collectivistic-influenced public school system. Last, but not least, an essential key to it all is a steady increase in suicide rates. However, in this new age, these obvious signs of suppression—clearly evident in all totalitarian-collective societies—are kept in balance by suppressants, through a steady increase of anti-anxiety medications and antidepressants (i.e., happy pills). Society becomes more and more deprived (in lack of ambition) and grows reliant upon the perfectly steady increase in entitlement benefits solidified through learned helplessness, successfully blinding society to the rapidly increasing collective oppression. This precise process of ambient socialism has taken place in the United States during the end of the twentieth century and continues to transpire ever more rapidly in the twenty-first century.

"Ambient socialism" or "universal welfare society" is democratically and fundamentally dependent upon mental equilibration through the weakening of society's general level of self-esteem—the necessary implementation of the severe inferiority complex. Without any doubt, socialism democratically is a slow subliminal, passive-aggressive process. It takes decades and generations to subdue the more independent right wing and create co-dependency to fully establish and achieve neo-communism. This describes the exact process that has slowly but steadily taken place over a 150 to 180 year span in Denmark, as well as throughout most of Europe. Rolled out over decades, this process ultimately achieves its goal of blinding society's citizens to think of this malignant collectivist mentality as an ordinary part of their culture.

Coercive Collectivist Societal Rules/Subliminal Conditioning (Malignant Narcissistic Coercion)

Don't question or criticize society, its citizens, or society's structure!

Don't express uniqueness!

Don't express individuality!

Don't express self-assurance!

Don't try to educate!

A truly liberated individual will quickly realize that collectivism's oppressive mentality is, curiously enough, the exact opposite of liberated. The inhibitions of severe pathological narcissism, "malignant narcissism," act to protect against all outside influence and to hold in place or eliminate any threat toward society's structure and collective way of thinking. Every individual is then slowly adapted throughout their upbringing to succumb to these coercive, narcissistic societal manners. Through the weapon of guilt, every person will impulsively and involuntarily police, guard, and defend the mentality's inhibitive rules in any way possible. These predictable and observable behaviors as a result of subliminal conditioning are also known in psychology as "psychopathic narcissism."

The level of the average person's understanding of this mentality is evidently determined by the level to which one has stood up against it. All Danes know that the oppressive collectivist mentality thrives. Yet in order for Marxism to prosper, it is vital that the truth never gets out. The best weapon to achieve this is magical thinking, either through absolute denial or by pretending that the mentality is a thing of the past. Many pretend to believe this mentality does not presently exist or that it does not truly affect them. Mistakenly, some even take the oppressive collectivist mentality (i.e., Jante Law), for an act of humility. While in truth, the gap between humility and the need to debase others is immense. Hypocritically, even collectivists hate this disclosed mentality. Yet when confronted with the facts, no one is willing to struggle for its discontinuance. One reason, besides personal feelings of inferiority, is that socialism, democratically, cannot survive without this mentality.

Totalitarianism describes a society coerced and completely controlled by some means of government. The Danish government is completely monopolized—as it acts in direct competition with private businesses—and gladly disregards any individual right, law, or constitutional amendment to control its population. Even so, in democratic socialism this authoritarian control is to some extent less carried on by the government, although the government is still a powerful coercive force. The near-complete force behind democratic socialism is in fact intellectual, the ambient emotional cold war for the vote, which gives the mandate to govern society.

A subliminal battle—Machiavellian egocentricity—subjectively achieving actions of imaginary generosity, which nonetheless are potent undermining measures that are controlled by co-dependency, merely to avoid confrontations or feelings of personal guilt.

Society's monetary lower-class masquerades as selfless altruists by using malignant narcissistic coercion (e.g., contemptuous behaviors known as shame dumping), to undermine, and thereby control, the stronger society. This is characterized by undermining for personal gain (i.e., means and control, which are perfected by superficial sympathy accomplishing enticement, utilizing the weapon of guilt, and calculating misuse of the message to care for society's weakest) and creating history's greatest perfected form of corruption—a mentality designed for one purpose only, which is to undermine the populace with the intent to radicalize society's otherwise confident right-wing individualistic voters, and thereby to keep complete intellectual control of the entire political democratic process.

AN EVERYDAY STORY

One day when I was in the process of buying a pillow in a shop in Denmark, I engaged in a nice conversation with the young lady who took my order. Since it was around noon, there were only a few customers in the shop. We spoke back and forth for about five minutes. As the girl handed me a plastic bag, telling me it was free of charge, a complete stranger walked by us. He overheard me say in a pleasant, conversational manner, "I am much obliged, as I do find it ironic that we pay the equivalent of fifty US cents, or more, for a plastic bag in supermarkets here in Denmark, bringing us Danes to pay an average of 140 US dollars annually simply for plastic bags. Having lived in Australia and the United States, I can tell you that in those countries plastic bags are usually free, and on top of that, they frequently pack the bags for you. Here in Denmark, we pay triple for everything and typically get no service in return." The complete stranger—a male who had been passing by—walked up beside me and shouted, "If you are not satisfied, then move to Australia!" He then quickly walked away.

Toddlers under the age of two can already perfectly manipulate by using their parents' love for them to coerce their parents, which accomplishes dominance by utilizing the weapon of guilt. This often causes problems for parents who are easily controlled by self-intimidation and are unable to process shame in healthy ways because of severe inferiority complexes that can cause anxiety. Therefore, these parents frequently give in to the child's demands. In some cases the roles of the child and parent, the strongest authority, switch places. These are the tools of guilt (projection, to accomplish co-dependency), that the monetary lower class uses in democratic collectivism to mentally overpower the strongest parts of society.

Imagine if every time you showed any signs of true individualism or confidence in yourself, your fellow citizens in some way intimidated you. With dominance as the objective, denigration is often disguised as reverse psychology or sarcasm, which is known as humor of the weak mind. You are slowly and systematically being mentally manipulated, preferably "conditioned" all through your childhood. In other words, you are undermined, intimidated, policed, preyed upon, and altogether subjected to ambient coercion in order to suppress your true individual self. This constitutes a form of stealth abuse known in psychology as ambient abuse, also known as gaslighting. You are indoctrinated to despise confidence, to lower your expectations, to never question or criticize society, to never be better than others, and to never stand out or be different from society's collective human organism and its goal: social equilibrium. Now weakened and feeling inferior, you are made to feel false contentment. You are blinded for collective suppression with fictive contentment, all of which is found in dependence upon society through the collective human organism and government bribery with entitlement benefits. This is Marxism's pathological mind game. Collectivism is using severe inferiority complex to create undermined human beings. Completely controlled by extreme pathological narcissism, they are programmed like robots to manipulate, intimidate, twist, and police-guard their societal surroundings. These malignant inhibitions are necessary to keep complete control of society, a society designed to use coercion, manipulation, enticement, and guilt as the main weapons. This creates a society in absolute need of suppressive coercion because manipulation, intimidation, and the weapon of guilt do not work on the strong mind.

"Socialism is a philosophy of failure, the creed of ignorance, and the gospel of envy, its inherent virtue is the equal sharing of misery."

—WINSTON CHURCHILL

CHAPTER THREE

A NEW WORLD DISORDER

Besides high concentrations of toxic fluoride, I have asked myself, in irony, if the Danish government has added something to the water supply; but then again, I choose not to believe much in conspiracies. I do, however, see corporatism as unconstructive, and if there truly is a conspiracy to create authoritarian corporatism—a new world order—I see only two ways to accomplish its creation. Absolute authoritarian mind control can be achieved through either fear or bribery.

Social equality is one way to ultimately achieve totalitarianism through democratic socialism. However, this passive-aggressive psychological approach is a slow option. The mental weapon of fear would undoubtedly be the quickest way to accomplish totalitarianism, which could be accomplished by spreading fear through terrorism, followed by disarmament, and ultimately a complete fascist military takeover. Threat and the fear of insecurity (i.e., crime and recession) allow authorities quick access to exceptional power of authority. To disable capitalism's market freedom, the global warming issue proves to be a great tool to promote totalitarian-collectivism.

Though I am not in denial of any likely effects of CO2, if studying the subject carefully one will factually find that the theories of global warming have not been proven. Climate change may be caused by factors other than merely human impact, and blaming people for global warming is a convenient tactic employed to undermine and control people through guilt. The theory of global warming is the perfect tool, misused by collectivists to apply rising (generally hidden) taxes, duties, and fees.

AN EVERYDAY STORY

Once in Denmark in a debate, a girl who attempted to manipulate by using the weapon of guilt started to enthusiastically explain with absolute excitement how she had held a public lecture at an educational institution using a PowerPoint presentation. People applauded when she proved that on a daily basis one million American citizens die from starvation. This girl's attitude is typical of a collectivist who is driven by severe inferiority complex and loathes Americans for their confidence. I laughed to myself, thinking, "I guess, were this true, then you will be overjoyed at the end of a year when the entire American population of a little over 300 million people has died of starvation."

Grandiosity is the diagnostic hallmark of pathological narcissism, also known in psychology as "superiority complex," which characterizes a superficial identity of superiority (a defense mechanism that occurs to conceal a person's inferiority complex). Conversely, radical collectivist narcissism to some extent disguises "superiority complex," and derives more or less entirely from "inferiority complex." Narcissism on the political left wing, therefore, is very different from autonomous narcissism.

One does not need to possess greater psychological understanding to realize that all people create their self-esteem through self-assurance, proving themselves, or being approved of by others. The Marxist, bound by oppressive collectivist mentality, is coerced not to express personal self-encouragement—a denial of the emerging individual self—so the Marxist suffers from unabated low self-esteem. This in turn disguises the "superiority complex." Driven by severe pathological narcissism, and to obscure these severe inferiority complexes, the Marxist creates a pathological illusion by utilizing the notion known as social equality—that all people are and should be treated equally—as an excuse to debase others. Marxists, and collectivists in general, alter reality through using magical thinking. An individual showing any sign of self-assured behavior, such as expressing oneself confidently, is considered self-absorbed. What in fact happens, when observed from the mind of the Marxist, is that signs of true self-assurance or self-encouragement trigger the Marxist's severe inferiority complex. In turn, this makes the person feel diminished. The ensuing result is a subconscious narcissistic response, an actual threat (a narcissistic injury), which creates an urge to intimidate, belittle, or humiliate. In other words: I feel like nothing, so you should too.

Since the collective narcissistic inhibitions are programmed from early childhood, these emotions of severe inferiority and the resultant pathological narcissism can be observed in just about all of the Danish population. Inhibitions, therefore, are created subconsciously and involuntarily. Consequently, the inferior, undermined person has very little understanding of, or control over, these inhibitive emotions. From a skilled psychological viewpoint, to find anyone in Denmark who shows genuine strong self-esteem is a truly rare experience. And with only one truly mentally liberated nation left in the world—the United States of America—no one has any other nation for comparison. Unlike in liberated cultures, completely normalized antisocial behavior can be observed commonly in all levels of society in Denmark.

While living abroad, I remember myself telling people that one is not able to easily differentiate between social classes in Denmark's almost completely equilibrated lower-middle–class society simply because, regardless of social status, Danes cuss constantly and lack courtesy and manners. This is the case even on children's television with its constant antisocial behavior, foul language, negative attitudes, and name-calling. Again, I offer this as an example of the lower-class's attempt to equilibrate themselves by purposely spoiling willingness for personal self-improvement by means of destroying the social ladder. Antisocial behavior is obscured by communizing it into society from early childhood, thereby spreading maladaptive behaviors into all societal levels. For what was otherwise considered low-class behavior is now normal. When the whole society acts like low-class people, there is no lower class anymore and no need for self-improvement to climb a social ladder that no longer exists. This allows perfect implementation of manipulism (denigration, projection, manipulation, enticement, and guilt), providing the necessary means for enabling the continuation of collectivism's equilibrating mental and societal assimilation.

I once read a joke describing the extreme inferiority complex facilitating social equality. A journalist had ended up in Hell. He looked around and saw great bonfires with big pots placed on top, one pot for each ideology in which people were boiling. Demons stood guard beside each pot, so no one could escape from them. Except, no guards stood by the Marxist pot. Thinking this was odd, he sought advice from the Devil and asked, "Why is the Marxist pot the only pot without guards?" The Devil replied, "No need for them! Should anyone try to pull themselves up, their fellow citizens will make sure to pull them back down again."

In order to truly understand collectivism, it is vital to understand that collectivism is a mental state created by the weak mind. The problem with social equality is that it is achieved through mental equilibration. It is not that society lifts the lower class, but that the lower class weakens society. The foundation that drives democratic socialism is low self-esteem—severe inferiority complex/pathological narcissism—that over the years, as radicalization progresses, spreads mental weakness, creating an epidemic that eventually reaches the farthest right-wing individualistic voters of society. This process of continuous malignant narcissistic coercion sadly deprives the very weakest of society's citizens, those without any ability to ever raise their self-esteem. This results in an endless denial of the individual self, those who are weakened to such extremes that they are driven by personality disorders, most commonly psychopathy and narcissistic personality disorder (NPD).

Severe pathological narcissism, which is now completely communized, again perfectly empowers the collective human organism progressively. Narcissists can now roam freely amongst society as ordinary citizens, further normalizing maladaptive behaviors into all societal levels and allowing society to live in an entirely altered reality, twisted by the collectivists' deprived state of mind. Antisocial behaviors are completely acceptable. Confidence is dreaded, and in fact, viewed as abnormal.

Narcissistic personality disorder (NPD) and antisocial personality disorder (ASPD) both involve the same cluster of characteristics found in psychopathy, thus the terminology "psychopath" in psychology is generally used to characterize antisocial personality disorder (ASPD). Psychopathy is similar in many respects to ASPD—characterized as a pervasive pattern of disregard for, and violation of, the rights of others; a pattern having begun in childhood or early adolescence and continued into adulthood—thus, psychologists have argued that most psychopaths meet the criteria for ASPD, while, most individuals with ASPD are not psychopaths. Hence, the more appropriate terminology to describe people with antisocial personality disorder (ASPD) would be narcissist-sociopaths.

Psychopathy is perfectly disguised by general public misapprehension, given that the general impression associated with the psychopath is violence and criminality. In fact, psychopaths are only rarely violent or psychotic. Standard in psychopathy, however, is the display of more cunning traits such as Machiavellian egocentricity, demonstrating pathological lying, being manipulative, superficial charm, living a parasitic lifestyle, displaying a calculated ability to regulate one's own behavior in order to exploit others for personal gain, in addition to a grandiose sense of self-worth, failing to accept responsibility for personal actions, blame externalization, and having unconcern for the feelings of others. Traits that are all ordinary in communists, socialists, and fascists.

According to the American Psychiatric Association's (APA) *Diagnostic and Statistical Manual of Mental Disorders* (DSM-V-TR), published in 2000, narcissistic personality disorder (NPD) allegedly appears in 0.5–1 percent of the general population. The APA's research is conducted on, and the statistics refer to, the confident American individualistic population. However, this research and statistical data are incredibly inaccurate in regard to radicalized collective societies.

Appropriate research must be conducted on collectivists. As well, careful analysis ought to be carried out on the general populations of Europe, including France, Germany, Holland, Italy, Greece, and particularly the Scandinavian countries. Such studies would demonstrate extreme levels of pathological narcissism in these countries, whereof a great part—figures likely as high as two-thirds—of the Danish population would prove to suffer from narcissistic personality disorder (NPD), with the most severe levels evident in the communist, socialist, and fascist parts of society.

Although the DSM has been used for set guidelines for psychotherapy in large parts of the Western world for more than thirty years, including Denmark and large parts of Europe, narcissistic personality disorder (NPD), curiously, is not recognized in Europe by *International Classification of Diseases* (ICD), published by the World Health Organization, located in Europe. Evidently, this is a necessary measure made to obscure the dreadful fact that collectivism causes mental illnesses. Areas of psychotherapy in radicalized collectivist nations of

Europe, therefore, generally use the IDC10 and refute narcissistic personality disorder (NPD). Of further curious interest is why psychotherapy in Europe's neighboring individualistic nation of the United Kingdom recognizes the mental illness. In England, narcissistic personality disorder (NPD) has even been used in forensic psychology for legal defense purpose.

However, regardless whether the disorder is recognized or refuted, with an average of at least seven easily observable narcissistic tendencies or more in the most radical collectivist parts of society, indeed extreme pathological narcissism (psychopathy) is the key to collectivism.

Narcissism consists of nine tendencies; an individual must demonstrate five or more to be diagnosed with narcissistic personality disorder (NPD).

In general assessments of narcissistic personality disorder (NPD), the autonomous narcissist, also known as a megalomaniac and characterized by superiority complex, expects to be recognized as superior without commensurate achievements and will debase anyone to ensure this superiority. The Marxist narcissist achieves these exact identical actions by means of exploiting history's utmost deceptive illusion, which is the notion of social equality—also known as social equilibrium. So rather than turning to "superiority complex" and expecting to be recognized as superior without commensurate achievements, the Marxist narcissist turns to employ "inferiority complex" and expects to be treated entirely equal without commensurate achievements, and will debase anyone, who by any means ever, appears or acts superior to the Marxist narcissist's extreme inferiority complex—what I choose to refer to as "inferiorlomania."

These general characteristics of "superiority complex" have been the primary assessments employed to diagnose narcissistic personality disorder (NPD). Consequently, by hiding in plain sight, Marxism has managed to evade detection for its entire era, camouflaged almost entirely by "inferiority complex."

Narcissistic Tendencies (Customized Radical Collectivist Traits)

Grandiose sense of self-importance, e.g., exaggerates achievements, skills, and talents to the point of lying; common projections of excessive moral superiority and takes for granted that others see this greatness; over-examines and compulsively corrects (policing) or downgrades other people, projects, statements, dreams, or achievements, etc., in an unreasonable manner

Preoccupation with success, e.g., fantasies of unlimited power (irrational ideals of achieving a perfect society with equal opportunities, entirely equal treatment, and elimination of poverty), brilliance, beauty, or ideal love, etc.

Believes that he or she is special, e.g., feels unique and only can be understood by, or should associate with, other special people or institutions (i.e., collectivists), etc.

Requires excessive admiration, e.g., gives overstated compliments for the purpose of personally prying in (e.g., the subject, the debate, or the other person), or for attention, affirmation, adulation; expects to be rewarded for appreciation in others (narcissistic supply)

Has a very strong sense of entitlement, e.g., demands automatic and full compliance with his or her expectations or holds expectations of unreasonable favorable treatment; feels entitled to other people's personal possessions (i.e., property, earnings, etc.)

Exploitative of others, e.g., interpersonality (chameleon), elusive, pathological lying; cunningly exploits the system, establishments, and people, etc., for personal gain

Lack of empathy, e.g., unable or unwilling to identify with the feelings of others, their needs, rights, property, preferences, and priorities, etc.

Envious, e.g., bears a grudge toward successful people of better psychological and economic standing, etc.

Arrogance, e.g., displays regular negative attitudes, haughty, snobby, compulsively judgmental, and opinionated; omniscient, highly conclusive about things in which the individual has factually no inside knowledge (magical thinking), regularly projects, tries to dump shame upon others (the weapon of guilt), and hypersensitive to criticism: rages when contradicted, confronted, or disapproved of.

All these inhibitive rules are hard to truly clarify, although there are two unwritten rules within the mentality that are in fact the easiest to explain. The first rule is in regard to a person who shows self-assurance or expresses one's achievements. This is in absolute breach of these narcissistic inhibitions. Contrary to this unwritten rule, these inhibited rules are not breached if an individual shows pride or confidence in oneself collectively or nationally, or otherwise as part of a group. Likewise, this rule is not breached if one utters approval of another individual's achievements or status.

The second rule, a truly deceiving yet absolutely vital dynamic in collectivism's pathological mind game, which blinds anyone who does not know the true nature/psyche of the collectivists, is that collectivists constantly seem to adulate. To a Marxist who has never expressed true personal self-assurance, cheering others is a subconscious prize. This excessive need for affirmation and self-love is referred to as "narcissistic supply." The basic subconscious thought being: I feel self-important; therefore, I expect to be rewarded for my appreciation of you. This seemingly kind gesture, or adulation, is required, so I can feel good about myself, indulge my grandiose ego, and embrace my high self-regard.

One thing that can therefore truly set off the collectivist's inhibitive emotions is encouraging oneself rather than adulating for reciprocal appreciation.

Viewed from the twisted mindset of the Marxist, and caused by excessive entitlement, lack of affirmation is considered inappropriate, self-absorbed behavior, which generally results in irritation, argumentation, and oftentimes name calling.

While at the same time as the attempt to equilibrate suppresses, a process exists that would, and does, create depression. Excessive collective affirmation attained through feelings of excessive moral superiority and self-importance, therefore, actually only makes up for the suppression created when demeaning and humiliating another's performance, professionalism, success, and happiness. Adulation is the collective human organism's constant attempt to keep harmony of this suppression. Excessive affirmation, or narcissistic supply, is obscured to the untrained eye, yet it simultaneously enables Marxism's collective human organism to be remotely in charge of society's co-dependency on a personal level.

"Analysis does not set out to make pathological reactions impossible, but to give the patient's ego freedom to decide one way or another."

—SIGMUND FREUD

CHAPTER FOUR

MANIPULISM AND THE WEAPON OF GUILT

Severe pathological narcissism and the resultant co-dependency lead the collectivist—who can hypocritically not take personal criticism—to turn one's attention completely away from oneself in an attempt to hide from one's impaired personal feelings and self-image. Instead, the person focuses one's attention on compulsively correcting (policing) and criticizing other people's behavior. The reason behind this, and the key to conformity, is that every citizen is their own imaginary police officer; therefore, to pry on others is overly common—truly ordinary even in public—often to the extent that it is encouraged and done with pride.

What makes a pedestrian in Denmark stop at an intersection at three o'clock in the morning while the light is red in the middle of nowhere without a car in sight? Imagine if the police only drove in undercover cars, then no one would ever know who the police were. This is exactly how collectivism works. When habituated slowly all through life, narcissistic coercion, policing and prying, combined with the resultant inferiority complex, creates anxiety from the sense of being under constant surveillance. One is held by an invisible force (Big Brother within) that stands guard against society's citizenry through self-intimidation, the weapon of guilt.

Oppressive collectivist mentality can be compared with a secret police group like the KGB or Gestapo. In Denmark, Marxists do not yet have an actual secret police that can eliminate the threat of the nonconformist. This is why severe pathological narcissism is so extremely dominant in Denmark. As mentioned before, because democracy in itself cannot radicalize collectivism, manipulism (malignant narcissistic coercion) replaces the Marxist's lack of oppressive fascist power. What is used here in a higher degree? The weapon under the USSR with the KGB, German Democratic Republic (GDR, commonly called East Germany) with the Stasi, and Nazi Germany with the Gestapo was to force guilt upon offenders. The cost would be great should an individual in Denmark break free from one's place in society. The Danish citizen who heard about an individual standing out in any way from the majority—by criticizing Denmark or by dressing or thinking differently—would coerce and force guilt upon the offender. Often passive coercion, resulting in self-intimidation, accomplished in public is achieved though silent projection, simply by staring. In the GDR after the fall of the Soviet Union, it was discovered that a third of East German residents had turned in a comrade, friend, relative, or spouse to the Stasi, the abbreviated name for the Ministry for State Security. This demonstrates the true power of guilt, self-intimidation, and spying used in socialism, communism, and fascism—all forms of collectivism.

1. Inhibition: Don't question or criticize society, its citizens, or society's structure.

Freedom of speech in democratic socialism, in reality stretches no further than the collectivist's right to denigrate other nationalities, lifestyles, traditions, or ways of thinking; hence, this in turn provides the necessary means for ensuring the continuation of collectivism's equilibrating mental and societal subjugation. However, hypocritical as collectivists are, freedom of speech never includes exposing the truth about them.

An untainted ideology is built on positive critique, as proof of its pure intentions. If one cannot write a ten-page criticism on the flaws of one's philosophy, one either has no philosophy or does not understand it. Surely, rather what one has is conformist authoritarian-collectivism.

Totalitarian behavior: Collectivists are indoctrinated to see absolutely no limit to authority and, as a consequence, do not question or criticize society. Totalitarian behavior goes hand in hand with malignant narcissism and relates to scornful envy, in addition to arrogance caused by hypersensitivity to criticism.

As well as being the strongest argument that supports disproving any claim that Denmark is the happiest nation on earth, this collective societal rule, which still results in life imprisonment in China and even the death penalty in totalitarian-collectivist societies around the world, would most undoubtedly be what makes collectivism so awfully dangerous. An inability to question or criticize society enables the state to do absolutely anything to its citizens. This fascist measure in a society like Denmark's is kept slightly in balance only by the center-left–wing social-liberal side of society. However, since democracy strips collectivists of their more preferable fascist approach, the collectivist is instead forced to turn to their second alternative: mental coercion. This, undoubtedly, is one of the easiest ways to prove how predictable authoritarian people truly are. Once having broken this specific inhibition, it takes only a few minutes—sometimes only seconds—to bring forth the collectivist's best defense. With almost no exceptions, when this particular inhibition is triggered, the result is a simple defensive expression that is repeated commonly in Danish society, so much so that one would think it has an actual Danish copyright. It has two forms, one declarative and one interrogative:

If you are not satisfied, then move away!

If you are not satisfied, then why don't you move away?

NOTE: Both examples are subjectively coercion. The second example demonstrates the reverse psychological approach.

This compulsive, coercive expression can be identified quite quickly as feelings of grandiosity: be like us, the collective human organism, or you are not welcome. This statement shows proof of the collectivist's excessive sense of entitlement, that society is all but fictitious solidarity, as well as proof of my theories of assimilation. Collectivists, co-dependent as they are, adopt words, statements, and phrases to achieve acceptance and to attain narcissistic supply—feelings of excessive self-importance and moral superiority—through being affirmed. However, this varies amongst numerous defensive expressions, e.g., "Opposing Obama makes you a racist." "Do you think you have the truth?" "Libertarians (right wing) only think about themselves." Some expressions are sometimes stated in a nicer way than others, but always the intention is reverse psychology with the purpose of intimidating and manipulating by utilizing the weapon of guilt.

This is a truly effective coercion when habituated all through life. Malignant narcissism (subliminal conditioning) creates an intellectual wall—the subconscious communist iron curtain—that perfectly immobilizes the critic from any criticism or questionability toward society. With almost no exceptions, this comment—impulsively triggered by an inability to process criticism naturally, excessive entitlement, and magical thinking—manipulates the critic away from the true subject and simultaneously enables the collectivist to move on by ending the conversation.

2. Inhibitions:

Don't express uniqueness!

Don't express individuality!

Don't express self-assurance!

All these inhibitive rules produced by feelings of severe pathological narcissism, which generate envy and the urge to feel equal, result in arrogance and excessive entitlement. This emotional process can generate narcissistic rage: malignant emotions of resentment, attitude, irritation, anger, and aggression. Narcissistic rage results in a subconscious narcissistic reaction: a sign of danger triggered when a citizen expresses self-encouragement or individuality. In fact, expressing self-assurance or individuality is a sign that the individual is lifting one's self-esteem, and at the same time, this is a true sign that the person is liberating oneself from the collective human organism.

3. Inhibition: Don't try to educate!

As already thoroughly described, collectivism generates a society that designs ways to indoctrinate its citizens—to maintain complete intellectual control of its citizens. Society is therefore perfectly designed—through the state-owned educational system, from daycare through university, and in large parts through the state-owned public media, by controlling what people are allowed to know—to keep people from gaining any insight into new and perhaps better perspectives or ways of thinking. This control extends to a need to prevent any foreign influence on society, and especially to prevent people from knowing the truth about narcissistic collective oppression.

What truly stands out as a vital part in creating and containing the collective human organism is therefore this exact rule: arrogance (magical thinking) disables anyone from teaching the collectivist the factual truth about collectivism's pathological mind game. This course has completely destroyed all natural respect for age and wisdom, and as well has destroyed the cognitive development process. As mentioned earlier, this personal story proves why totalitarian-collective societies restrict information and the right to travel.

To prove my point, when claiming that collectivists believe that they always personally know best, I only have to refer to this rule. However, this omniscient arrogant attitude is actually not imposed because collectivists believe that they themselves truly know better. It is simply their subconscious, deprived narcissistic defenses, hypersensitivity to criticism (an inability to process shame in natural ways), and magical thinking that create this arrogant behavior.

What is truly deceiving is that, in reality, the radicalized collectivist members of Danish citizenry portray themselves as the nicest people in the world. That is, of course, only possible until one observes or triggers their psychological disadvantages. Raising your voice just the tiniest bit, in fact even the least bit of excitement, will often trigger the collectivist to feel intimidated. A radicalized person can be your best friend one moment and your worst enemy the next. Unpleasant behavior, arrogant attitude or narcissistic rage, is in most cases emotionally triggered by the least bit of disapproval, contradiction, or exposure to undesired facts and insights. Once the animosity is released, this person will often try cunningly to befriend you again a split second later.

Largely influenced by appearing superior to the collectivist's sense of worth, the collectivist will display grandiose feelings of self-importance. This inhibition against superiority (excessive entitlement) is commonly triggered when an individual tries to explain or educate a collectivist. Reading about or hearing information contrary to the collective thought results in the undermined person intuitively displaying excessive moral superiority: attempted coercion though projections, utilizing the weapon of guilt. On the other hand, these emotions of severe pathological narcissism can be withheld, but this is only likely to happen if (1) the collectivist sees some benefit for personal gain; (2) the undermined person has personally taken the first step by showing interest or asking directly (however, by referring back to point (1), this is usually the cunning attempt to manipulate or use reverse psychology); and (3) the individual who breaks these inhibitive rules is someone of unique status (e.g., a teacher or a tourist vacationing in Denmark).

Excluding these emotions results in a truly deceiving yet absolutely vital dynamic that blinds anyone who doesn't know the truth about the collective pathological mind game. After all, a collectivist will never reveal collectivism's negative aspects. Even though my birth language is Danish, for purposes of researching the language barrier I often speak English when I go out. To some extent, speaking English allows me to be me because a collectivist will not treat a potential convert in the same way as someone who is already a part of the collective human organism. After all, Marxism is the world's newest religion (doctrine). In fact, socialism has replaced religion in Denmark, where less than 3 percent of the Danes practice religion. Instead of praising a higher power, Danes seek complete contentment through the entitlement benefits and narcissistic supply achieved throughout the collective human organism.

AN EVERYDAY STORY

A great example of how easy it is to trigger the collectivist's inhibitions of inferiority is the story of when I invited my brother and an American friend along on a ski holiday to the French Alps. Midweek, a snowstorm hit the mountain, and all but one beginner's slope was closed. My friend came up with the idea that to use our time best, he would teach me how to snowboard. My brother chose to stay behind, and we went to snowboard. A little under two hours later, my friend and I, two proud boys, returned to the rented apartment and enjoyed the afternoon by talking about how quickly I had managed to master the snowboard. The joy only lasted a few hours because my brother exploded in frustration over the continual encouragement he had to witness. My brother's typical collectivist narcissistic behavior created such a resentful atmosphere that we barely spoke the rest of the holiday.

Keep in mind that we are talking about my brother, who of course is forced by the family relations to have a higher tolerance than the average collectivist friend or acquaintance.

The theory of manipulism can be divided into three categories of coercion. The first is direct and obvious, through contemptuous manipulism; the second is cunning and obscured, through sarcastic manipulism; and the third is reverse psychological manipulism. The creepiest of the three is reverse psychological manipulism. It is characterized by attempted enticement, in other words, by utilizing what is best known as the Svengali technique, ambient abuse, or gaslighting. Here, the collectivist narcissist, at first and with cruel intent, portrays oneself as a sympathetic person by pretending to be curious about something, e.g., the subject, the debate, or the other person. He or she demonstrates this curiosity by inquiring into specifics or private details. However, should you be an open individual and reveal any personal information about yourself, then the collectivist will use these against you. In an attempt to manipulate you, the collectivist will now use "you" against you, with the intent to create guilt as an instrument of persuasion. The Marxist collectivist narcissist tries to use the value of their opinion as a tool of impact, considering this subconsciously to represent the collective human organism. All this is as a result of what, in their fantasized sense of moral superiority, is not being social. Of course, regardless of the argument, social is always in regard to the Marxist's own personal gain and need. This truly is effective exploitation of the frail mind, and it is especially effective on a collectivist, whose personal ego is in fact a collective identity.

The social-psychological theory of manipulism is used in various ways. The military uses techniques similar to the ones used by the narcissist in collectivism to form a perfect human organism first by breaking down the soldier's mental state, and after that by building up the soldier's self-esteem. Through collective punishment, and by means of setting up soldiers against one another, military officers achieve a potent personality sphere—coercion among the soldiers—that binds the perfect compliant unity. This technique effectively transfers the soldier's contentment, which the soldier then finds in his or her weapon and reliance on the troop.

In the case of domestic violence, a situation that is always subject to severe pathological narcissism, abusers control the abused by lowering their self-esteem with verbal or physical abuse. The abused is eventually driven by feelings of severe inferiority and co-dependency. So even after the abuse is finally filed with authorities, the abused will frequently drop the charges due to emotions of guilt and the need for contentment. The contentment of the abused is now found in co-dependence on the abuser. This state of mind is referred to as Stockholm syndrome.

Complete authoritarian mind control by means of manipulism has been proven to be achieved quite quickly and is often seen in small communities, cults, and sects. These community groups are always subject to one of the most dangerous types of psychopathic characters—the psychopathic narcissist as well as the cold and calculated narcissist-sociopath—who cunningly exploit the frail mind for personal means and power. To the untrained eye, narcissists and narcissist-sociopaths can easily portray themselves as considerate, concerned, and compassionate. Sociopaths are people who are known to avoid doing crimes by their own hands (e.g., Adolf Hitler, Joseph Stalin, and Charles Manson), as sociopaths are generally so cunning and persuasive that they con others into doing their crimes for them.

The narcissist is always in search of frail minds, ready to provide narcissistic supply, and always ready to take part of a shared psychosis, a *folie à deux.* To protect their ego boundaries and by means of setting up one against another, narcissists create a potent personality sphere around themselves (the sect) that operates as a perfect compliant unity. Repeatedly, methods of manipulation, ambient abuse/malignant narcissistic coercion is used (e.g., Jante Law, tall poppy syndrome, schadenfreude, etc.), creating a shared psychosis, from the size of two, to a family, to a whole country, living united in their sensation of vanity.

Narcissist cult leader David Koresh of the former Branch Davidians establishment in Waco, Texas, managed to implement manipulism through misusing religion for personal gain by acting out sickening sexual desires including sexual assault, statutory rape, and bigamy. David Koresh attained complete mental control over his followers in less than a quarter-century.

The Peoples Temple, run by the narcissist cult leader Jim Jones, also managed to attain complete control over his followers in less than a quarter-century. Jones did so through socialism and his misusing of the word of God. Again, he acted to satisfy his needs for personal gain, including securing power and fulfilling his appalling sexual desires. Using undermining, authoritarian mind control, his community consequently ended with a terrible outcome in which more than nine hundred people committed mass murder-suicide. Group think, known as the lemming effect, doomed the Peoples Temple.

In both preceding examples, with no deviation from the conduct of a socialistic-influenced government, the process of implementing manipulism appears to be straightforward. The subject portrays oneself as thoughtful, kind, and sympathetic. This facilitates an ability to symbolize oneself as a role model, custodian, or caretaker. A human organism is now slowly formed about the subject, creating followers who promote the cause and its objective. The subject will eventually manipulate the prey to volunteer personal possessions, goods, and assets, and thereby to be cared for by the community—utilizing these personal possessions, goods, and assets to gain further power, while slowly stripping the individual of all civil liberties. Soon, tools that undermine are implemented, enabling dominance and the weapon of guilt. Eventually, followers are mentally prevented from criticizing by means of bribery, authoritarian coercion/ denigration, spying, and intimidation of self and each other. The creation of a sect has been accomplished.

Both previous examples resulted in Stockholm syndrome, in which people factually defended their subjugators though subconsciously they knew they were being abused; irrational, but like the Danes, they still present themselves as joyful.

"None are more hopelessly enslaved than those who falsely believe they are free."

—JOHANN WOLFGANG VON GOETHE

CHAPTER FIVE

A STATE OF PSYCHOPATHY

It is probable that you have known of the collectivist mentality since childhood, as your parents are likely to have read out loud the world-famous children's story released in 1843 written by the Danish author Hans Christian Andersen, *The Ugly Duckling*. The story is thought to be his personal way of describing how society made him feel, living undermined by, and subjected to, the maligned societal norms that prevailed all over Europe in the nineteenth century's then conservative society. And similar to radical collectivism, in conservatism, everyone has an exact place in society. This suggests that similar conformist conservative norms must have already held society in place.

AN EVERYDAY STORY

While living in Australia, I once meet a Danish couple who had had enough and, therefore, had immigrated. To define the Danish collectivist mentality, one of them stated, "Danes will run a key over the finish of your brand new Mercedes just to state their dissatisfaction with your unequal social status!" The previous story did not really come to mind until I moved back to Denmark. While in my stay here of less than five years, I have gotten burn marks in two expensive coats while out nights on the town. In addition to meeting a young Danish male one night in a bar who, without any knowledge of the previous story, actually told me about an identical experience of someone who scraped a metal gadget, likely a key, all along the side of his brand new Mercedes. He expressed this incident as the reason why he now votes as far right as possible in Danish politics.

When understood, the universe of psychology is a universe of true mental freedom. Self-esteem and self-confidence are linked, yet they are very different. Self-esteem is somewhat passive and not always easy to detect. Someone with low self-esteem can easily appear confident. Self-esteem describes an individual's general subconscious perception of one's own worth: the individual's perception of oneself and how the individual believes others see and feel about him or her. Self-confidence is dynamic and describes motivation, willingness, and the ability to interact socially.

The human need for socializing, forming friendships, and conforming to society becomes one of collectivism's strongest weapons. The collectivists stand together as one by utilizing the weapon of guilt, accomplishing dominance, using their friendship to coerce, and excluding or denigrating anyone who is in any way critical toward collectivism.

There is no doubt that people in a country like Denmark, at some point in their lives, stand up against this tyranny. But due to the great need for friendship and acceptance, eventually everyone compromises and ultimately succumbs to collectivism.

In fact, being liberated by high self-esteem proves to be a disadvantage since those who are independent and liberated are not as organized. Individuality is the exact weakness of the right wing. In contrast to the more independent right-wing, the collective human organism has the power of many. They feed off each other's narcissistic supply: feelings of excessive moral superiority. As a result, when the majority of society's citizens are first undermined by severe pathological narcissism, it is nearly impossible to win back a political balance. This political balance can only be achieved through will and insight. In short, balance can be accomplished only by psychological means.

Unless the collectivist has actually lived abroad individually for many years, and so has had the opportunity to absorb different cultures, lifestyles, and behaviors for comparison, the person has no means to know any difference and lives with absolute ignorance of the truth. Such people are outwardly unaware of the societal coercion, as well as their severe inferiority complexes that keep them subjected and denigrated. This person will simply react upon them subconsciously either when these rules are broken or when threatened with the truth.

It personally took me almost ten years of traveling, observing, and researching all over the world, while building self-esteem, before I truly started to understand. This demonstrates exactly how strong and powerful the emotional iron grip of collectivism truly is.

This is the exact reason why I feel I can make my next claim: there is no such individual as a truly liberated Dane. If one searches sufficiently enough, one will spot in every Dane a hidden collectivist in any supposedly liberated individualist. Regardless of experiences, everyone in Denmark is in some way compromised by the collective human organism.

In fact, if your first thought was denial of that claim you just read, I offer this curiosity to make myself quite clear: even I am affected, though I have submitted myself through years of self-analysis and educated myself both sociologically and psychologically. Not keeping silent makes it extremely hard to live here. To speak up or attempt to break free of these inhibited societal rules only leads to constant clashes. Revolt only results in complete societal abandonment.

Actually, while writing this book I lost family and collectivist friends, people with whom I have been friends since childhood. In collectivism, you convert or you pay. In reality, you pay anyway. I am likely to lose even more, but in any struggle for change there must come pain, sacrifice, and hardship for a greater value.

One will undoubtedly find plenty of people deprived by narcissism around the world. And as anyone who has actually had an encounter with a narcissist already knows, the experience is undoubtedly unpleasant. However, in a more liberated culture like America's—because the average American, at least for the time being, has a moderate to strong level of self-esteem—the average individual does not put up with antisocial behavior, making self-improvement vital to climb a social ladder. This suggests why the United States has more serial killers. Besides collectivism's usual cover-ups or poor investigative police work, antisocial behavior is universal in collectivism; therefore, the maladaptive narcissist is disguised. As a consequence, the narcissist can easily blend in with the rest of the frail populace, giving him or her a much-needed facility for socializing. In contrast, in more liberated cultures the narcissist is quickly singled out and left alone to oneself. This important sense of separation is essentially impossible in collectivism, where society thrives commonly amid maladaptive psychopathic behavior. Eventually, the liberated individual will simply remain passive and say nothing—perfectly driving the continuance of collectivism.

To accomplish social equilibrium and the necessary societal assimilation, it is of utmost importance that there be a true slayer of individualism. Enslaved by oppressive collectivist mentality, the collectivist feels bound to find one's personal self-esteem elsewhere. There are only a few ways for one to establish self-esteem. One of the most common ways is found through sports. This can also be achieved through narcissistic supply, emotions of moral superiority, and collective affirmation, or by replacing one's self-esteem with nationalistic feelings.

The Danish youth, in general, is almost in competition as to who is the best at speaking English—generally American English—some with an almost flawless Americanized accent, which for Denmark's bystander and visiting tourists makes Danes stand out as well educated. Yet, having a debate with a well-educated Dane about even the simplest facts about politics will show a completely different story. Controversially, the reason why these people speak English as well as they do is because this is one of the few places where one can actually evade Marxism's societal rules in secret, thereby allowing sensations of high self-regard by subconsciously declaring aloud, "I am better than you," without actually stating it directly.

In contrast to viewing or treating one's fellow countrymen no differently than any other human being on earth, regardless of standing, race, or nationality—in my view the description of a true individualist—nationalism, where one is devoted to the country's people, race, bloodline, and land, which in this case the Danes have lived on for millenniums, is therefore an awfully powerful collective force; hence, sensations perfectly utilized in fascism (e.g., Hitler's "Nazism"). Besides being an absolute slayer of prejudice and racism—caused by chauvinistic feelings of being superior to other races, nationalities, and nations—nationalism is an absolute necessity for success in accomplishing collectivism. No more so than the way we aid people in third-world countries, should people in the Western world have any special treatment or the right to vote themselves to someone else's assets simply because they share the same nationality. National feelings, nonetheless, provide fictitious solidarity—an essential superficial loyalty—misused by the Marxist to obtain projection (the weapon of guilt) and socialism's favorable treatment.

Collectivism is only psychological mind-control made absolute through the exploration of the most universal and basic human need: contentment. And what makes collectivism so truly notorious, and the reason why it is absolutely essential to keep people from feeling completely content within themselves, is that collectivism attempts and accomplishes, through the means of manipulism, to destroy individuality by completely replacing the individual's self-identity with a subconscious collective identity.

Since the Marxist collectivist narcissist is seemingly kept from expressing self-encouragement, which is obvious and enhanced by superiority complex in the often deeply haughty autonomous narcissist—grandiosity is therefore somewhat disguised in democratic socialism through a false sense of humbleness. Believing themselves to be humble, subdued by severe pathological narcissism, Marxists alter reality by seldom expressing self-encouragement. The twist, though, is that the Marxist turns to chauvinism. In addition to the female Marxist who turns to extreme feminist chauvinism, the Marxist turns the narcissistic trends into encouraging excessive collective and national admiration. Identified in virtually all forms of collectivism, even though each trend is felt collectively, the feelings are the same: fantasies of collective and national superiority.

As a result, no matter how hypocritical it may sound, suppressive collective mentality purposely allows the Marxist, who is otherwise seemingly not allowed to feel superiority, to feel grandiose and self-important by demeaning or criticizing other nationalities, lifestyles, traditions, or ways of thinking. Marxists, and collectivists in general, are inclined to reject that any other nation could be even slightly better or at least on equal footing. This allows the collectivist to distort reality and create a falsified self-esteem via excessive nationalistic affirmation. Thus is national collective admiration, or narcissistic supply, achieved through feeling superiority over other nationalities. By replacing their low self-esteem with strong collective and nationalistic feelings—a collective ego, "a madness shared by many," also referred to in psychiatry as "shared psychotic disorder"—collectivists have once again empowered the unity and assimilation of the collective human organism.

Anyone can properly relate to rooting for one's team or sharing a united team spirit with other team supporters. Yet to collectivists, the feeling is so intense that the accomplishment feels like one's own. Indeed, everything Danish is seen to be superior—hospitals and education, food and customs. It is worthless to attempt to persuade Danes otherwise, and virtually impossible to do so. Identical to religious people who worship God, Danes worship their country; and they even place the national flag, similar to a religious symbol, on birthday cakes and Christmas trees.

Truly annoying is the Danes' excessive and constant need to talk about how wonderful Denmark is and how much better we Danes are and our nation of Denmark is compared to other places. Excessive collective admiration (magical thinking) results in arrogant conclusions that are generally constructed from assumptions rather than from actual knowledge. All of this is part of a pathological mind game to completely disable any skepticism, questionability, or criticism toward authorities or society's structure. And with half the service levels at a cost of living that is at least double, and more generally triple, that of the United States' prices, one could ask rhetorically whether these people are deeply delusional.

Narcissistic Tendencies (Collective Narcissism and National Chauvinism)

Grandiosity and self-importance, e.g., exaggerates national or collective achievements, skills, and talents to the point of lying; takes for granted that others see this prominence (e.g., immigrants or tourists); downgrades other nationalities, lifestyles, traditions, or ways of thinking, etc. in an unreasonable manner

Preoccupation with success, e.g., fantasies of brilliance (nationally or ideologically), or beauty (e.g., Danish women are the world's most beautiful; Danes are the world's most intelligent, etc.)

Believes that he or she is special, e.g., feels unique and can only be understood by, and should only associate with, one's fellow countrymen and collectivists, i.e., feels nationally superior to immigrants and other nationalities

Requires excessive admiration, e.g., displays nationalistic and moral superiority; takes for granted that others see this greatness; expects adulation, attention, or affirmation (narcissistic supply); expects to be rewarded by tourists and immigrants with national and moral admiration, etc.

Has a very strong sense of entitlement, e.g., demands automatic and full compliance with his or her expectations; has expectations of unreasonable favorable treatment (e.g., over third-world people, "starving Africans," or newcomers)

Exploitative of others, e.g., interpersonality (chameleon), elusive, pathological lying; cunningly kind to tourists, etc., all for collective and national promotional gain

Lack of empathy, e.g., unable to or unwilling to identify with the feelings of other nationalities, lifestyles, preferences, priorities, traditions, or ways of thinking (e.g., the Muhammad cartoon crisis)

Envious, e.g., bears a grudge toward successful nations of better psychological and economic standing; resentful toward newcomers, i.e., fugitives, receiving equally entitled benefits, etc.

Arrogance, e.g., displays regular negative attitudes, haughty, snobby, compulsively judgmental, and opinionated; omniscient, highly conclusive about other nations and nationalities in which the individual has factually never been to or has inside knowledge of (magical thinking); projects regularly, tries to dump shame upon others (the weapon of guilt), and hypersensitive to collective or national criticism: rages when contradicted, confronted, or disapproved of.

Marxists, and collectivists in general, misuse their message, but will do anything to persuade mankind otherwise. They masquerade as humanists, and selfless altruists, and as those who care for society's weakest. However, collectivists totally lack empathy. While this emotion, or rather lack of emotion, is generally hard to observe, collectivists are completely irrational and cunning. Collectivists are driven by tremendous sensations of self-righteousness. A collectivist's high self-regard, envy, arrogance, and entitlement, driven by severe pathological narcissism, completely take over emotionally. In reality, the only empathy Marxist narcissists have is what relates directly to their personal needs and desires.

Marxists have a complete lack of rationality (magical thinking), which therefore results in an absolute lack of empathy. However, Machiavellian egocentricity is employed by framing their motivation through superficial sympathy as care for society's weakest—as a tool of projection (the weapon of guilt) to dump shame on others. This not only allows the Marxist to feel morally superior—in addition to creating a personal pathological illusion by diverting the truth away from personal self-interests and co-dependence, which ultimately allows the Marxist justification for exploitation of society for personal gain—but also creates a perfect illusion of being empathetic.

Referred to in generic terms as egomaniacs, psychopathic narcissists and narcissist-sociopaths lack empathy. However, narcissists are not necessarily sociopaths, yet sociopaths are always narcissists. The sociopath, who is often the result of traumatic childhood events such as excessive neglect, physical or mental abuse, or incest, is completely unable to feel remorse or identify with feelings of others, whereas the psychopathic narcissist can. Narcissists have strong emotions; however, their empathy stretches no further than their ego. Anything is disregarded except what they can identify in themselves or what involves their self-pity or personal needs. They feel love and therefore protect themselves from feeling less worthy by means of mental coercion. They will continuously drag other people into their deprived pathological mind games, using illusion and methods of ambient abuse to distort reality and truth. They achieve intimidation by degrading and demeaning others in frequently cunning and obscured ways, thereby spreading mental illness by lowering society's self-esteem, thus achieving co-dependency. All this suffices to endlessly nurture Marxism's collective human organism, the world's biggest sect.

Collectivism is history's utmost elusive criminal mind game, created by a syndicate of self-pitying parasitical narcissists who feel excessively entitled. They so much believe themselves to be right that they presume the authority to force their views upon others. It has resulted in an infinite evil circle of emotional terrorism. Those who foster manipulism are masters at creating puppeteers who in turn create more puppets. The puppeteer is the collectivist's everyday occupation.

Were it not for the fact that narcissism—named megalomania prior to when narcissistic personality disorder (NPD) was first formulated by Austrian-born American psychoanalyst Heinz Kohut in 1968—one might wonder if "Nazism," a contraction of national socialism, was not in fact misspelled.

"Socialism only works in two places: Heaven where they don't need it and hell where they already have it."
—RONALD REAGAN

CHAPTER SIX

THE ODD ONE OUT

When the German theorist Karl Marx in 1848 published *The Communist Manifesto*, he overlooked a critically vital error in his theories: personal boundaries. The simple fact is that humanity always consists of people who will feel the need to be liberated, people who feel the need for absolute independence and individuality. It is absolutely necessary to suppress this freedom of thought—the essential conversion of individualism's healthy personal boundaries into collectivism's bad boundaries—if collectivism is to succeed in creating an equilibrated human organism. Unless all citizens voluntarily participate, collectivism is tyranny. Full non-manipulated participation would create utopia. It is therefore a necessity for Marxists and fascists to take these despicable mental manipulation techniques into practice or use them for direct physical control of society, or both, as seen in former Nazi Germany, former USSR, Cuba, China, North Korea, and several countries in South America. In these countries, thousands of individuals, the nonconformists, are forced to flee to avoid being imprisoned or murdered in honor of collectivism. And we must not forget the nonviolent Tibetans and their Dalai Lama, who are either prisoners of, or fugitives from, Marxists.

It is true that some modern-age Marxists (e.g., Fabian socialists), portray themselves as in favor of democracy. Thus when individuality is first completely replaced with a collective identity (bad boundaries), and therefore under complete societal control, the person is yet another link in the collective human organism. When society gets closer to its objective, communism (totalitarianism), the organism decides and not the human being.

Bad boundaries, precisely the severely narcissistic trait in which the very principles of collectivism have their origin, are responsible for the collective unity holding society's members accountable for one another. Yet this does not take into consideration that one has no right to evade personal responsibility by holding others accountable for oneself. Bad boundaries can be seen in contrast to the indisputable personal right of claiming independence. Of course the latest excuse for oppression is fictitious solidarity and democracy. However, in large part, the democratic process is sooner or later determined by deprived, parasitical voters with no interest in politics except for what can be personally gained. They not only determine the fate and limit the rights of others, while not contributing to society themselves, but also decide the country's future economy and consequently the country's economic destruction as well.

Although narcissism is malignant self-love—the need to control one's surroundings, bad boundaries, and a continuous search for narcissistic supply (mirror mirror on the wall, who is the fairest of them all), adulation, attention, or affirmation attained from one's surrounding community—this is quite the opposite of the individualist, the independent thinker resting within oneself. Thus, collectivists often go as far as to misinterpret (e.g., normative egoism), the need for independence and individualism as narcissism.

The collectivist believes oneself to be so right, driven by a grandiose sense of self-importance—a sense of entitlement so strong that one's beliefs should be forced upon others—without any deviation, which is always the result of severe pathological narcissism. In contrast, the confident individualist believes in personal independence: that one's ideals are personal and therefore do not apply to others, no matter how strong one's personal sense of entitlement.

Society, being the mere extension of the collectivist's identity as a result of bad boundaries, creates the perfect pathological narcissistic sphere. Observed from the collectivist's state of altered reality, anyone who in any way appears confident or superior to their grandiose ego and anyone who does not meet their needs, share their views, comply with their plans, or willingly provide narcissistic supply—all traits of the confident individualist—is viewed as the odd one out and as having an inconsiderate, self-absorbed, and egocentric personality. A twisted reality, endorsed by grandiose feelings of collective unity (make-believe empathy), allows the collectivist to twist self-interests into a pathological illusion of generosity and unselfishness. Bad boundaries (magical thinking) perfectly engender the need for independence to be viewed as egotistical. Fantasies of excessive moral superiority create the perfect pathological narcissistic sphere that perfectly empowers the collective human organism through adulation, attention, or affirmation: narcissistic supply.

AN EVERYDAY STORY

I was once at the ticket office at Denmark's State Railways purchasing a train ticket to Sweden for a business meeting, when the female cashier handling my order started belittling the Swedish Public Railways in an attempt to attain narcissistic supply from me, through national affirmation. I looked at her and started to explain, "If you want to throw stones, I sincerely hope you can take reverse criticism, so let me enlighten you about your own employer." I went on to explain that I had once been kicked off a train, though I had an absolutely valid ticket, simply because the female ticket inspector wasn't informed about the new ticket type I was carrying. The ticket inspector issued me a fine, which didn't worry me as it would, of course, be canceled as soon as the issue was resolved. The female inspector asked for my Danish Identification Card, which I then handed her. She looked at the ID for a moment, then handed me a paper form for writing up the fine. She demanded that I write my personal details. I declared that if she wanted to give me a fine, I could deal with that, but I was certain the issue would be cleared up once she found out about my ticket type. I said, "If you want to give me a fine, you write it." The female inspector looked at me angrily and said, "If you don't do as I ask of you, I will kick you off the train at the next station." I denied her demand to fill out the form and was kicked off the train. Now finished telling my story to the cashier, I further explained to her, "Having lived for many years abroad, I can tell you that services in Denmark are not the greatest in the world. And if you wish to hear more awful stories about your own employer, I'll be happy to inform you." The cashier looked angrily at me and started telling me off, while handing me the ticket that I had just bought. She ended her words the exact same predictable way as all Danes in general, "If you are not satisfied, then move away!"

In collectivism's pathological mind game, mental coercion is beyond calculated. As mentioned before, this is because it is generally disguised even though it is inevitably constant. The game always takes a negative approach. The humor of the weak mind is sarcasm, and it is used constantly to disguise denigration. I recently engaged in a pleasant conversation with a waitress in a café, when her unaffiliated boss, for no apparent reason, approached me and said, "I wish you were a radio, so I could turn you off." Similarly, every time I would proudly announce that I had met a new girl, my brother would instantly say, "Is she blind?"

Just like seemingly harmless sarcasm is used to disguise contemptuousness, so is reverse psychology. Instead of making the usual direct attack such as, "You have some personal issues!" a collectivist narcissist will generally use the reverse-psychology approach, "You have some personal issues, don't you?" This, Svengali technique, is truly effective on the frail mind. This approach allows the narcissist to slowly enter and manipulate the selected victim's mind, thus creating coercion by utilizing the weapon of guilt.

A simple, commonly used remark like, "Don't think you are anything!" is not always noticed consciously, especially when it is expressed sarcastically and habitually delivered all through life. However, subconsciously, the story is very different. When I started writing this book I considered naming it You Can't! This seemingly innocent comment, a compulsive response, always as a result of low self-esteem, is one of the most common expressions used in collectivism's pathological mind game. Because after hearing, "You can't!" enough times, seemingly innocent comments like these quickly become powerful, detrimental psychological undermining. This is especially effective when used on the frail mind.

In an attempt to undermine the confident individualist, any cruel extreme is used. Personally, I have been accused of many things, ranging from being told, "You should be on medication!" to "You must be borderline!" As well, I've been subject to the creepy reverse-psychological approach with questions like, "Do you take medication?" or "Do you have ADHD?" Some have even gone as far as calling me a psychopath, and the list goes on.

Quite definitely, these typical collectivist allegations meant to stir humiliation, intimidation, and belittlement, did hurt me. As a result, they made me question myself. Fortunately nature's gift to me was the ability to always be truly observant; therefore, I always strive for a better self-understanding. For that reason, I had already sought counseling for the first time in my mid-twenties. In counseling, the first pieces of the puzzle were placed into position. So except for the clear signs of schizoid disorder (a personality disorder characterized by a lack of interest in social relationships, thus, the signs ironically only occur around collectivists), and although these ruthless souls attempted to achieve otherwise, there was absolutely nothing abnormal about my personality. Yet the emotional iron grip of collectivism, which subjected me to years of tormenting, would prove to have an additionally powerful stronghold and prove to be not easily broken.

All of these attacks directed toward me represent examples of truly effective, calculated, detrimental narcissistic coercion used to keep the individualist in line. You are as you are persuaded. Having been undermined and made to feel inferior when I was in my teens, I often felt like the odd one out. I would have been convinced by every word I was told, and my self-esteem would be no better than that of all other Danes, if it were not for the fact that I moved to the United States, where people acted like individuals, behaved confidently, and spoke openly, exactly like me.

For the last twenty years, I have gone on seven-mile runs about three to four times a week. And while living abroad I began to sing along to music while running because singing allows me to detach and feel unaffected by my surroundings. However, in Denmark things are different. In Denmark, hostile bystanders persistently intimidate me by staring, laughing, and yelling at me. Therefore, in combination with almost three years of therapy and the intent to finish this book, I have just about succeeded in completely liberating myself from any collectivist intimidation. In this time I have been able to observe and analyze the therapist, eventually reaching the conclusion that she as well was driven by pathological narcissism.

In fact, this is when the collectivist's predictable mental narcissistic defense cheats them by altering reality and thinking of this behavior as odd. "Why would I want to run and sing?" they ask or think. However, this behavior is odd only to people with low self-esteem. Deprived egos keep them from feeling comfortable with running and singing. I can kindly suggest that one stops lying to oneself. The point here is not whether one likes or wants to run and sing, but if one actually can.

The frequent misuse of terminology, like "You're arrogant!" amongst other condemnations, is a major part of collectivism's pathological mind game. The collectivist's intent is dominance, to coerce and force guilt upon any individual who expresses oneself assured. This imaginary reinvention of terminological definitions is caused by magical thinking (omniscient illusion), simultaneously making the collectivists who use the terminology stand out to the uneducated as well educated. Although, collectivists actually use attacking terminology, being deeply and ignorantly arrogant, they can seldom clarify a simple term like "arrogance." Most interestingly, if confronting collectivists with their arrogant behavior, they will in fact react with arrogance.

The inferior mind alters reality, thus it is truly important to understand the difference between unhealthy narcissism and the freedom of expressing confidence in oneself and one's achievements in healthy ways. Arrogance, which is expressing pride for the purpose of feeling superior to others, is quite different from a healthy ability to express self-assurance. Self-encouragement and self-recognition are exceptionally important psychological needs to build individuality and personal endeavor. These traits are significantly important for opposing unhealthy narcissism by combating those who denigrate others for expressing themselves as self-assured. Always keep in mind that only the inferior mind has the need to debase others, which in turn subordinates society.

Narcissists are drug addicts in need of their daily fix, and their drug is narcissistic supply. Demeaning or humiliating others makes narcissists aroused and creates a subconscious high that makes them feel better about themselves. This malignant self-love allows the narcissist to obtain adulation, attention, or affirmation: narcissistic supply. Being admired, feared, or affirmed by others is like a drug for the narcissist. This is especially effective when encouraged collectively. Like an instant drug, demeaning others gives the narcissist a momentary strong self-regard. This fix briefly provides forged confidence to persons who are otherwise truly neurotic.

As well as having been in a long-term relationship with a partner who was driven by severe pathological narcissism, which initially spiked my interest and research in narcissism, I once went on a few dates with a narcissist. This relationship was very short term though, as once she explained her often-used technique for seeking joy by irritating her former partner. She purposely irritated him and created arguments to make herself more sexually aroused for intercourse later.

I once heard a wise and appealing story concerning the topic of the oppressive collectivist mentality. It goes like this: A Dane was describing how, while in the United States, he felt inspired by the American attitude. While in the process of elaborating on this, the collectivist noticed the American nodding oddly, seemingly agreeing with the topic. When the man finished explaining, the American smiled and said, “Great, good for you!” Surprised by the comment, the Dane asked, “What do you mean by that?” The American then replied, “If everyone in your country is so preoccupied with not believing in themselves, then there is just so much more room for your success.”

The gap between being self-assured and worshiping oneself—severe pathological narcissism—is not immense. However, the example above of the uplifting, uninhibited liberated behavior (benign envy) and the right to be self-assured and express oneself freely is a vital psychological tool for all of society to employ to create self-esteem and individualism. Many Americans have no clue that this encouraging mindset is the mentality that is the actual force behind anyone who has success. The belief in the American Dream is the motivation that drives Americans to succeed, and their positive striving is the world’s strongest economic force and influence on success. Liberated mentality, self-assured behavior endorsing strong self-acceptance—individuality—is the weapon against collectivism.

Liberated Mentality

Embrace disapproval; question society, its citizens, and society's structure!

Embrace uniqueness!

Embrace individuality!

Embrace strength!

Embrace self-assurance!

Embrace curiosity!

The fact is that the oppressive collectivist mentality drives people to live a dependent life of envy. Amongst some collectivists, envy is so predominant that one can have a feeling that the collectivist knows what is in one's bank account before oneself does. The liberated mentality is very different; it encourages the individual to turn one's envy into being observing, outgoing, questioning, and encouraging (benign envy) by gathering inspiration and motivation in individuals of a better intellect and standing. These successful individuals are those who believe in themselves and encourage others who strive to reach the same level of accomplishments. This contrasts greatly with the oppressive collectivist mentality. Individualism creates a positive psychological cycle. This is what I refer to as America's Social Security, the shoulder clap of encouragement that raises the levels of self-esteem for all of humanity.

As a consequence of this constant support, the nation of the United States, which is built on benign envy—the shoulder clap of encouragement—in combination with market freedom, has not only shaped the world's largest Gross National Product (GNP) but also the most millionaires, and in fact billionaires, in the world. Most importantly, this upper-class wealth has placed the American middle class in the world's top five. So even though the American middle class is not ranked the first—

with the scarcely high income taxes, sales taxes, and generally hidden duties and fees applied in all top-ranked countries—the American middle class is among the world's most prosperous.

China, the country that has the world's second largest Gross National Product (GNP), which averages US 5 trillion dollars, accomplishes their position as an economic power with a population of approximately 1.3 billion people, versus the United States' GNP averaging over US 14 trillion dollars, which is accomplished by a population of only just over 300 million people. The United States has nearly triple the GNP with a billion fewer people creating that wealth. This offers more than enough prosperity for even the slightest opportunist willing enough to take part in the climb to accomplish the American Dream, and in addition this offers clear proof that absolute liberty, capitalism, and non-government intervention is the only true source of success.

Weapons against collectivism to teach your children and others:

How others see you is beyond any doubt insightful. Though, the true importance is how you see yourself. Avoid comparing yourself to others.

Approval from others is beyond any doubt positive. Yet, to find individual approval within is always of the highest priority. Never compromise your individual self.

Always listen and be curious and observant. Use benign envy to find inspiration in self-assured individuals who believe in themselves and lift their surroundings through encouragement.

Regardless what is said or done, no one can put you down. Only you can put yourself down. Avoid debasing yourself by referring to or thinking of yourself with denigrating statements.

Always encourage and express confidence in others. Especially embrace others in expressing self-encouragement and self-assurance in themselves.

Our mistakes do not define how bad we are, but merely how much better we can become. Anything in life can be turned into a positive.

By no means ever underestimate the manipulative strength of the narcissist. They are stronger than you anticipate. Psychopathic self-love knows no bounds. To protect their ego-boundaries, the narcissist will manipulate, cheat, lie, steal, and even kill. In short, they will use any means available within their reach to protect their frail egos from exposure.

Feelings of guilt are often closely connected to tools of the narcissist. Therefore, always examine your feelings carefully for false pretenses.

Keep your distance from people who are compulsively judgmental and opinionated and from those who express excessive foul language, negative attitude, and envy, especially people who deny responsibility for personal actions and lack the ability to take criticism.

Furthermore, it is important to understand that Marxists are truly hypnotized by the belief that they are doing good with what they stand for—all smoke and mirrors. This is perfectly disguised by their magical thinking, “I am a selfless person who cares for others.” These ideals create the perfect facility for self-deception—deceit from self-interests. One would easily argue that a selfless person is not someone who takes from others by force and thereafter shares it around—the description of a tyrant—but that a selfless person is someone who personally makes and voluntarily shares one’s own private assets and time.

To care for others is without any doubt an indisputably beautiful philosophy. Yet self-deception from a narcissistic ego can be somewhat easily identified. Socialism would in fact not work democratically were it not for personal gain. This blinds Marxists to the fact that everything refers back to their personal co-dependence, their lack of personal initiative and self-pity. As a result, Marxists try to bring down their environment to their level of achievement—feelings of inferiority, unmet needs, and fear—which then drive them to turn their envy, and often their feelings of communal neglect, into resentment and anger directed toward those who are better off. In other words, envy sets up a pattern of using people of a better psychological and economical standing as their scapegoats.

It is most important that one understands the two-rule remedy of economics (non-bureaucratic involvement and the free market), and of equal importance, to understand the significance of upholding liberated mentality. Then, in any way you can, stand up against these ruthless souls and their constant attempts to denigrate, twist, and project the weapon of guilt upon the independent thinker by preventing the individualist from expressing individuality and self-encouragement, the truly liberated way. Hence, rather stand out from the flock as a black sheep than follow suit in the crowd as a tiny lamb.

"Before you diagnose yourself with depression or low self-esteem, first make sure you are not, in fact, just surrounded by assholes."

—STEVEN WINTERBURN

CHAPTER SEVEN

THE LAND OF INFINITE EXCUSES

I have traveled for many years and have been fortunate enough to visit more than thirty countries. Also I have lived in three countries for a length of time, which has given me the chance to truly observe, analyze, and understand these countries' cultures and customs—finally with concrete knowledge for comparison—allowing me to observe my country from a completely foreign point of view.

Out of all the people of the more than thirty countries I have visited and observed in my lifetime, America's individualistic populace undoubtedly rank number one in high emotional intelligence (EQ). Australia is undoubtedly one nation of which citizens most openly demonstrate obvious signs of entitlement/narcissistic rage. Severe narcissism is truly obvious in the fiercely aggressive, apathetic Australian driving culture. The sensation of security attained in the confinement of a vehicle frequently brings forth the true mental state of the driver. In Scandinavia, narcissists are harder to spot to the untrained eye because Scandinavian collectivists in general—being truly subjugated—are in awe of authority and, therefore, absolutely compliant—in large parts to the extent of appearing impassive—opposed to Australia's rebellious Aussies. While both cultures demonstrate overwhelming behavioral and mental similarities, Scandinavian collectivists are undoubtedly among the world's most deprived.

One would think that a country's government benefits would have no sufficient importance when studying the psyche of a country's inhabitants.

On the contrary, my research showed when Danes are asked to identify specifically why a statistic ended up nominating the Danes as the world's happiest, Danes in general refer instantly to the almost unlimited entitlement benefits. Though the majority of Danes plays the lottery on a weekly basis, curiously a common expression used among collectivists is: "Prosperity doesn't make happy!"—thereby refuting the assertion that happiness cannot be purchased. In the case of the Danes, fictive happiness is purchased with entitlement benefits—conversely, a happiness facilitated by prosperity. This further demonstrates how easily government entitlements can replace actual happiness with falsified contentment, perfectly blinding all to the malignant collectivist oppression.

A few refer to feeling safe and secure—apprehensive as the general population is—as well as the inability and lack of personal rights to defend oneself or one's property. These, however, quite clearly prove to be misapprehension.

The gap between being provided for and genuine happiness—found in emotional contentment—is truly immense. Denmark is a bearable place to live for as long as one does not actually have an opinion about reality. And I am not referring to collectivized city-mentality when I declare that these collectivists barely recognize each other's existence. When observing these supposedly social people—the world's supposedly happiest populace—in their personal comfort zone, the majority proves not to think an inch beyond their own ego. So except of course for the entitlement benefits, which creates the illusion of sympathy, empathy is scarce to nonexistent. Nearly no one voluntarily offers a seat to an elderly, pregnant, or disabled person on public transportation. The most deprived people smoke to calm their anxiety and have absolutely no qualms about smoking within a few feet of children. Collectivists rarely smile and are very reserved, to the point that one may even find them rude. Collectivists in general are very skeptical and suspicious, preferring to keep to themselves—to the extent that large parts of the citizenry act like hermits.

Recently, while on a run, I gently excused myself at a distance to pass a couple in their fifties blocking the narrow path on which I was jogging, when the male, who was walking a German Shepherd, literally jumped into a bush. Though I am an absolutely properly and nicely dressed male, when I kindly offer assistance or attempt to make a conversation (e.g., at the bus stop or in public transport), I unintentionally spook collectivists fairly easily—frequently resulting in a backlash caused by their inhibitions. Collectivists, deprived as they are, live in a comfort zone, severely inhibited as a result of their having a hard time declaring that one doesn't want to confer. This comes as a result of self-intimidation (the inability to process shame in natural ways); this again aggravates them. Even the kindest remark is often instantly viewed from a negative approach. Greeting a neighbor or having a conversation with a stranger—even in a bar, a club, or in public—happens, but it is not necessarily very common. If so, the barrier of inhibitions is generally broken with alcohol or other intoxicants.

When passing each other in public (e.g., at the supermarket, on public transport, etc.), rather than excusing themselves, collectivists, self-absorbed as they are, will simply bump into people or squeeze their way through. Though the most evident and easily observable lack of empathy is seen in the way Danes will wait behind you or your children and expect to be noticed rather than showing common courtesy by pardoning themselves. The phrase "excuse me" is very rarely used.

To feel content, the truly neurotic people often need to walk on a specific side of the sidewalk or sit on the exact same chair (e.g., at the cafeteria, at work-gatherings, or every time one attends a lecture at an educational institution). When using public transport, one can observe people sitting on the outer seats or placing items (such as a handbag or jacket) in the seat next to them—subconsciously aware that most fellow collectivists are neurotic too, therefore, they don't have the courage to ask for the vacant seat. So unless they feel it is their last option, they would rather find somewhere else to sit, or they will simply stand. Collectivists rarely ever sit down next to strangers in the public space. Thus, in parks, one can observe them sitting alone at park benches. And just like in parks, buses and trains will fill with people sitting in seats as far apart as possible.

Performances like these are easily observable anywhere in Denmark. Anywhere in the world, in fact, these severities of collective subliminal suppression, and depending on radicalization, can be measured through the extent in which these easily observable inhibitions occur in the public space. Hence, cultural freedom and individual choice, individualism, will show as self-assuredness, curiosity, and openness; whereas collectivism shows as emotional distress (e.g., anxiety, neuroses, and reservedness), which in turn can be seen in physical distancing. In other words, freedom brings people together while collectivism pulls people apart.

AN EVERYDAY STORY

Ten months had I waited, unable to do any sports, when the day for my surgery finally arrived. Due to the free medical system, I had been waiting for about nine months since being diagnosed. The minor surgery in my knee went exceedingly well, and I was out of the hospital in less than half a day. Since I was armed to the teeth on painkillers, I chose public transport. Crippled as I was I got on the bus, as best I could, yet I was barely on before the bus driver closed the doors and took off. I clutched myself on to the nearest pole, and from there I fought my way to an area of the bus prioritized for wheelchairs and strollers and sat down on a fold-open seat. I could have sat in a seat nearer to the front if not for the fact that young people occupied the seats originally reserved for disabled, pregnant, and elderly people. The bus made two more stops before a woman with a stroller boarded and needed to occupy the area I was sitting. I therefore moved. Still not one person offered me a seat, and I stood the rest of the way. Finally, the bus came to my stop, but if enough were not enough, now whilst exiting the bus the driver literally closed the doors on me. And to end the tale perfectly, when passing the doors at the front of bus, the bus driver opened the doors and turned toward me and said, "I didn't see you because you got out of the bus so slowly."

Words are only relative and factually proven to mislead. Those who suffer from pathological narcissism alter reality and portray themselves as content. When persuaded by self-deception (magical thinking), collectivists can be truly convinced of their happiness—yet subconsciously, they feel the opposite. A statistic of happiness completed through surveys is therefore questionable, regardless how thorough the questionnaires.

When trying to analyze happiness, one would observe individual psyche—observations of people's personal performance in their comfort zone: driving performance, signs of aggression, anxiety, openness, hospitality, courtesy, satisfaction, and dissatisfaction. This is especially the case if individual happiness, subconscious contentment, is based on materialized contentment, such as possessions and money, opposed to non-fictive emotional contentment.

Publicized statistics from 2006 (according to *World Map of Happiness* data), show that the Danes are the happiest people in the world, and I am quite convinced that the statistics are correct. That is, if they are to be established on the fact that the Danes truly believe they are the happiest people on earth. Nonetheless, when observing behavior, especially when comparing suicide rates, which are a scientifically undisputed symptom of suppression, a completely different reality emerges.

Alcohol consumption is over the top in Denmark. The Danish youth has for years been ranked as the largest consumers of alcohol in Europe. For the average Dane it takes a six-pack to find relief from inhibitions and get on the dance floor. Danish young people, who are often very insecure from resultant anxiety caused by severe inferiority complexes, need drugs even to attend an exam. According to the data (from *European School Survey Project on Alcohol and Other Drugs*), Danish adolescents still rank as top consumers of drugs and alcohol.

Beyond doubt, to be deprived of one's true individual self makes people mentally ill. The majority of Denmark's citizenry ought to be in therapy—deprived emotionally by collectivism's constant narcissistic tyranny (subliminal conditioning), which in most cases of truly deprived persons leads to clinical depression. As a result, prescriptions for antidepressants (happy pills) are overly common; in other words, those who begin to see and feel will use drugs or abuse substances to suppress their emotions. According to (*Organization for Economic Co-operation and Development* data), Denmark factually rates the second highest consumer of antidepressants in Europe, only surpassed by Iceland. In reality, if it were not for the widespread use of antidepressant medication, which is tremendously diminished in price by government subsidization, Denmark's suicide rate, last published in 2006, (according to *World Health Organization* data) of 11.9 per 100,000 would rank at least double, though likely triple, the level of today. Denmark's suicide rate—with an average of 20.8 per 100,000 during the last five decades—reached its highest level of 32 in 1980 and has since slowly but steadily declined by 1 per thousand annually. This statistic is in relatively perfect harmony with the increase of antidepressant usage over the last two decades. Compare the Danish suicide rate to the rates for the individualistic cultures of the United Kingdom and the United States, whose small suicide rates have been nearly perfectly steady. United Kingdom's suicide rate last published in 2009 by WHO of 6.9—with an average of 8.5 during the last five decades—has never exceeded 10.7. The American suicide rate last published in 2005 by WHO of 11.0, with an average of 11.1 during the last five decades, has never exceeded 12.7.

As evidence that collectivism thrives on oppressive narcissistic coercion, leftism always has its strongest iron grip in denser populated areas, as opposed to rural locations. Further evidence is the pattern of the high suicide rate that repeats itself in totalitarian collectivist societies, as well as suicide rates that frequently rise steadily all through life. This can be seen in contrast to more liberated nations, with comparable climates to Denmark's and far less entitlement benefits, such as Denmark's neighboring countries of Great Britain. In this individualistic culture with virtually the same climate, the suicide rate is relatively minor; the suicide rate reaches its peak in midlife and progressively drops.

Seasonal weather, more precisely lack of sufficient sunlight, can unquestionably contribute to depression. Weather can, however, only contribute as a trigger. Weather in no way causes depression without coercion or isolation. The isolated Danish island of Greenland has a suicide rate that is exceptionally high, but it still accounts for a mere fraction (approximately twenty-five annual suicides) of those that make up Denmark's estimated seven hundred annual self-inflicted deaths. Greenland, the biggest island in the world, is populated by only 56,000 people.

In regard to depression, statistics from 2012 (according to the *Danish State Serum Institute* data) show that 455,000 people were prescribed antidepressants, a number that has nearly doubled since the statistics were first published in 1999. Today's average represents more than 11 percent of just over 4 million Danish adults—of the supposed happiest population on earth—factually reported to be using prescribed antidepressants. One could make a joke: "Well of course Danes are happy; they are medicated to be."

Suicide rates would unmistakably have been rapidly on the rise in the individualistic cultures of the United States and Great Britain if not for the invention of antidepressant medication. Consumption of suppressants in the United States according to US data (from *Centers for Disease Control and Prevention*) and from United Kingdom data (according to the *London School of Economics and Political Science research*) have increased excessively in perfect harmony with the progression of democratic socialism, that being the influence of the Democrat party in American politics and the Labour Party in British politics.

Denmark has truly become a Prozac nation, medicating its way out of malignant collectivist oppression. As the collectivist's last resort, it has even been widely accepted to medicate children from early childhood. Often those medicated are in fact misdiagnosed children who rebel and do not know that they actually rebel against the undermining of their true individual selves, their right to express themselves naturally, and their basic right to individual liberty.

If accurate statistics were to be established for a country's level of happiness, then one should compare rates of self-esteem, suicide rates, and statistics for usage of antidepressant medication, taking into consideration whether a country's citizens can afford this medication. Most importantly, statistics would have to take into consideration that a liberated mentality not only permits criticism toward society but individualism embraces this tool, along with benign envy—confident self-encouragement and selfassurance—as absolute vital psychological dynamics. Collectivist mentality is the exact opposite. Therefore, instead of the title "the happiest people," the Danes are more appropriately labeled "the most spoiled," having been destroyed mentally by collectivism.

Should anyone seek a role model for a social society, radicalized collectivist societies would undoubtedly be the last place to look. The social consciousness that collectivists attempt to promote is nothing but severe pathological narcissism, and displaying bad boundaries is the exact opposite of social culture. On the surface, Marxists would seem content—like birds in a cage—yet beneath the surface, they are anything but social and are in truth far from happy. Of course, the exception is being social and happy in regard to sharing other people's money.

By now I should have established that people, in fact, can have a blissful life in democratic socialism—until the government eventually, as always, runs out of other people's money. One can argue that this utopian lifestyle exists for as long as one takes from life, without question, and without any kind of critical or realistic opinion. The only problem in collectivism is that individualists like me, who do not want to participate in the tyrannical system, are not given an equal choice. In fact, to this day, no higher form of discrimination exist than the notion that all people are and should be treated equally.

I do occasionally ask myself why I still live in Denmark. Quite frankly, no community offers a better environment for social observation and analysis. A genuine freedom enthusiast with insights, who is in pursuit of objective and subjective independence, and who can manage to rise above the injustice, ignorance, and collectivist coercion, can accomplish anything. Only a collectivist puts up with collectivists. Undoubtedly, no better self-control or anger management exists.

"Three things cannot be long hidden: the sun, the moon, and the truth."
—BUDDHA

CHAPTER EIGHT

PYSCHOPATHOLOGY AND THE TOOLS THAT RARELY LIE

Collectivism can be defined by two words: bad boundaries. Having bad boundaries is defined as the inability to understand, or unwillingness to respect, personal boundaries. This can be seen in contrast to individualism, which is characterized by healthy boundaries, personal tolerance, or the ability to understand and respect differences—to respect the individual's right to personal choice, regardless of personal principles.

Collectivism goes hand in hand with stripping people of their individual rights. With any collectivist in office comes the drive for control of society. An infinite number of laws and regulations will be passed, growing and empowering the bureaucratic government further, and thereby limiting personal freedom by the minute. A recent attempt to further strip the Danish people of their freedom of individual choice can be seen with the Danish socialist government mandates in 2012 that proposed a law enforcing Danish parents to read bedtime stories to their children. This illustrates the perfect everyday-life example of democratic socialism and the severity of narcissism (bad boundaries) that drives collectivists. A collectivist is absolutely ready to strip anyone of their right to individual choice; for a collectivist, anything that feels or sounds right for them must also be right for everyone else.

The reason why the oppressive collectivist mentality originally caught my curiosity was that I found in my early observations that the farther left wing a person casts one's vote, the more intense is the severity of their pathological narcissism. Today I differentiate between the collectivist and the individualist only through observing signs of narcissistic traits. Collectivists are master manipulators, pathological liars, who in almost unlimited various ways not only try to mislead those around them but also live in an entirely altered reality that allows them to convince themselves of their own deception. Only when one is really convinced of one's own lies can one truly persuade others to believe those lies.

Marxists, and collectivists in general, can create any pathological illusion. Using wordplay such as "solidarity" as justification for tyranny and the exploitation of the general public, or using terminology such as "tax" to justify extortion, perfectly allows collectivists to twist reality, utilizing this wordplay perfectly, as the collectivists' pathological mind game. Moreover, by referring to democratic socialism as "welfare," or affixing the word "social" on a word, or introducing "social" in a sentence (e.g., socialism and social-liberalism), collectivists can create misperception of being or feeling social. Modern collectivists have distorted the term "liberalism" as can be seen with Marxists referring to themselves as liberals, while in reality they support intentionally growing government control as well as limiting the liberties of the nation's citizenry. Thus, "liberals," collectivists, contradict the very basic principles of liberalism, which among other descriptions is defined by freedom and equal standing under a non-intrusive government. Social liberalism, or liberal socialism, a perceived ideology, is a great example of these numerous Marxist attempts at twisting the truth. Marxists use liberalism as a camouflage, thereby enabling them to implement totalitarian-collectivism.

The opportunities to delude are plentiful and work perfectly on the frail and ignorant mind. Thus, only the psyche is relevant. After using the tools given in this book and having some practice with them, and given a few minutes of observing behavior and narcissistic traits, anyone with modest insight into the psychological tools of pathological narcissism will be able to identify a person's level of self-esteem—the severity of the person's egocentrism/narcissism—and thereby pinpoint where this person likely votes on the political scale.

NOTE: *In consideration for the developing ego in adolescents and younger children, for a psychiatric diagnosis of narcissistic personality disorder (NPD) or antisocial personality disorder (ASPD) to be given the person must be no less than eighteen years of age. The undeveloped personality lacks independence and may be swayed through coercion to embrace the ideals of parents, friends, and society. Therefore, it is generally recommended not to use these tools on people who have not yet reached their late twenties.*

Whether the parties identify themselves as left wing or right wing, the whole of the Danish Parliament is a body of collectivists. The Danish Parliament includes eight political parties of Parliament spread out over the entire left wing (from communists, socialists, and fascists to social liberals)—all of which perfectly represent the political spectrum and voters facilitating the entire Democratic Party in America—each and every one a collectivist party that operates in breach of personal boundaries. Thus, having created an imaginary right wing, Denmark's farthest right politics are what most of the Western world would deem center-left wing. Denmark, therefore, creates the perfect facility for social-psychological research, with each party allowing social observations of their unique variations in psychopathy, narcissistic traits.

Psychopathic narcissism is seen frequently in collectivists—likely in more than two-thirds of the population—scattered over the entire left-wing political scale. Of course these figures refer to a society that has achieved neo-communism, such as Denmark's. Without a strong political right wing and the subsequent liberated mentality to embrace benign envy—the shoulder clap mentality that encourages self-assured behavior endorsing strong self-acceptance—the interminable collectivist suppression is immense.

Accordingly, averaging at least seven easily observable narcissistic tendencies, the most severe form of pathological narcissism, psychopathic narcissism, is easily identifiable on the (radical) left wing in the deeply arrogant and scornfully envious, working-class communist and socialist parties. This sadistic behavior (malignant narcissism) expresses the true characteristic of extreme pathological narcissism. With expectations of being treated entirely as equals without mandatory achievement and entirely unable to distinguish between self and society, these narcissists frequently even dress in accordance with their equilibrium and inferiority-complex fantasies, so as not to appear better than anyone.

Being an academic in democratic socialism only defines what it is to be well educated in anything that does not contradict the core principles of Marxism. The socialist-democrat party—with their ideals of entirely equal opportunities for all without mandatory achievement—is frequently facilitated by voters who hold higher academic degrees.

And as a result of better education, socialist democrats frequently appear self-assured. These highly self-regarding and high-flying narcissists, consequently, can often easily disguise their excessive self-importance and truly arrogant and scornfully envious behavior since the symptoms of severe pathological narcissism frequently elude the untrained eye.

While all communists and socialists turn to chauvinism (grandiose sensations of nationalistic or moral superiority) to create a "shared psychosis," a *folie à deux*, the national socialists, also knowns as national fascists—although, definite socialists—stand out from other socialists. National socialists, similar to other socialists, in fact believe in social equality. However, national socialists—being rationally motivated—believe that only certain superior races, groups, or nationalities are entitled. National socialists utilize "nationalistic feelings of superiority" and create broad politics extending all over the left-wing scale, from the far-left left wing (communist and socialist politics) to Denmark's imaginary right wing. This makes them quite different from all other socialist parties that every so often turn to employ nationalistic feelings of superiority but generally favor the more elusive feelings of chauvinism. Socialist parties—including the communist party—generally turn to employ "excessive moral superiority" (Machiavellian egocentricity) by utilizing superficial sympathy and the weapon of guilt through framing their politics as to care for society's weakest. They do so by means of blame externalization by dumping shame on the "farther right" political parties, and so, create a *folie à deux*. A potent political personality sphere is achieved through narcissistic supply, shared fantasies of excessive moral superiority. High self-regard is attained throughout the far-left left wing's collective human organism through preoccupation with succeeding at developing the perfect utopian society without any poverty, where all people have equal opportunities and are treated entirely as equals. They desire to accomplish all this while, most importantly, enabling socialist and communist parties to appear empathetic, generous, and thoughtful—the perfect pathological illusion of superficial sympathy—disguising their true tyrannical intent.

Socialists utilizing "sensations of moral superiority" are indeed very different from the national socialists (who favor politics spread across the entire left wing) and tend to lean on the left wing's imaginary right-wing collectivist politics. Consequently, they are hindered to some extent from utilizing chauvinistic tools of excessive moral superiority. As an alternative, they turn to obvious prejudicial politics: often chauvinistic hate tactics and blame externalization, such as racism. Narcissistic supply is achieved through chauvinism—generally collective "feelings of national superiority"—allowing national socialists to create broad politics all over the entire left-wing scale.

There exists an erroneous perception that Hitler, a national socialist, and his hateful collectivistic, fascist ideals of national supremacy were aligned with genuine individualistic right-wing politics. Ideals perceivably used by Hitler's national socialists have often been referred to as "right-wing authoritarianism" (big government and control), though one might see this as an oxymoron. The truth is that there are extremists and chauvinists everywhere on the political scale. What I find mind-boggling is how ideals built on right-wing cornerstones (individualism, small government and personal freedom) and patriotism (being loyal to the success and future of one's country) in its extreme form—undisputedly being ultimate freedom and even lesser government—ever ended up as an oxymoron of totalitarian collectivism, big government, and collectivist feelings of national superiority (the devotion to the country's people, race, bloodline, and the earth). Thus, one cause, among others, for this twisted worldwide misperception that the national socialists were genuine right wingers is the ability of the national socialists to grab politics from almost anywhere on the political scale in conjunction with the invention of the imaginary right wing on the political left.

With collectivism's attempt to succeed at creating social equality, utter societal assimilation truly has been accomplished. One of many results of which is severe pathological narcissism. Severe inferiority complexes have led to extreme chauvinistic feminism, where Marxist women have become fiercely masculine and almost androgynous in appearance. Marxist feminists often divorce their husbands in search of independence, yet they remain dependent, marrying the government the next day. Feminist chauvinists, or feminazis, are often in rejection of gender roles, and are entirely controlling of their surroundings, so much so that it has more or less emasculated the Danish males. Forget the Vikings. This explains my wife's impression of Danish men when she first met me. She often expressed confusion at the Danish male's emasculated appearance and behavior, which in absolutely no way is meant as an attempt to denigrate Danish men, but she literally thought most Danish males were homosexuals. Feminist chauvinism has gone so far that one is likely to receive a backlash when acting a bit conservative and gentlemanly enough to show a kind gesture such as holding the door open for a woman.

The Radical Socialist Party—the farther right socialists—is generally occupied by feminist chauvinists as well as by voters of higher academics, similar to the Socialist Democrat party. This socialist political party is, however, unique: unlike the farther left left-wing socialist parties in which females dress more womanly, the farther right socialists tend to appear androgynous. As well as being dissimilar, being that this is the first political party on the left wing's imaginary right wing—these socialists deceitfully portray themselves as liberals—employing a combination of the usual socialist sensations of moral superiority, thus generally portraying themselves as better at economics. Although, more curious is the unique change in behavior on the political scale of extreme pathological narcissism. This is demonstrated by a slight change in their narcissistic tendency of arrogance, by a tiny transformation from the usual compulsive denial to a minutely more observant behavior.

Supporters of the further right, which are Denmark's center-left—wing collectivist parties—the social-conservative party and social-liberal party—all show clear signs of pathological narcissism, though severities vary. Thus, severe levels of pathological narcissism are frequent. On the whole, levels of pathological narcissism tend to be slightly more moderate. The excessive malignant narcissism (scornful envy and arrogance) found on the farther left wing, consequently, appears to be replaced on the imaginary right wing with contemptuousness, negative attitude, or haughty behavior. Hence, across the left-wing spectrum of the Danish political parties, projections are still frequent.

In the farthest right collectivist politics, and Denmark's newest potential political hope, founded in 2009, lies the farthest right party in Danish politics. Thus, roughly three-quarters of the voters are collectivists, generally social liberals deprived by obvious, though generally moderate, levels of pathological narcissism. While believing themselves to be right wingers, only one-quarter of these political voters make up Denmark's actual somewhat centrist group. These people still have the urge to clarify themselves excessively when confronted with reality or with being wrong, which is a significant indicator of the inability to process shame in healthy ways. This lack of responsibility for errors is the reason why the left wing deserves the title, "magical thinkers of infinite excuses." Oppose this to the truly liberated mind—the mind of a person who comfortably accepts criticism and acknowledges personal mistakes.

Severe pathological narcissism—the oppressive collectivist mentality—is completely obscured by the deception that one-quarter of the Danish populace, the farther right socialists (radical socialists, social conservatives, and social liberals)—the imaginary right wing—refer to themselves as liberals. This allows society to live in the perfect pathological illusion that the collectivist's maladaptive behavior and severe inferiority complexes are normal. In addition, the collectivist's excessive sense of entitlement—the inability to distinguish between self and other (bad boundaries)—perfectly establishes the misapprehension that confident self-encouragement and self-assured right-wing individualistic curiosity, openness, and criticism is to be perceived as abnormal. I have personally met no more than about twenty to thirty genuine freedom enthusiasts in Denmark. I believe that out of the roughly 5.5 million people that make up Denmark's entire population, the actual number of individualistic right-wingers does not exceed 30,000.

While all radical collectivists are indisputably driven by pathological narcissism, collectivists can be categorized in two ways as assessed by the inability or unwillingness to recognize personal boundaries: (1) truly mentally deprived persons—communists, socialists, and fascists driven by extreme pathological narcissism (bad boundaries) who are completely unable to distinguish between self and other, and can be referred to as subjugators; and (2) collectivists—the imaginary right-wing's social conservatives and social liberals—who are driven by moderate to high levels of pathological narcissism, and are unwilling, rather than unable, to recognize personal boundaries, and who can be referred to as subservient, radicalized by society's egomaniacs, and therefore, coerced by self-intimidation and mentally subdued by anxiety, co-dependency, and personal feelings of guilt.

This is not to say that libertarians, "true liberals"—known in present times as "classical liberals" renamed by the collectivist's modern socialist liberal deception—can't have low self-esteem or be driven by severe pathological narcissism. Signs implying low self-esteem are often racism and prejudices. Easy signs for the untrained eye to observe in identifying higher levels of pathological narcissism are (1) the inability to distinguish between self and other, (2) the inability to process shame in natural ways, (3) the inability to act responsibly upon personal actions, and (4) exploitation of others for personal gain. These can be seen as contrasts to signs of high self-esteem such as being curious, open, observant, positively self-critical, and outgoing in general.

AN EVERYDAY STORY

Just after the Danish election in 2011, I attended a public victory meeting held by Denmark's newest political party, the center-left wing and farthest right in Danish politics, to celebrate the party's arrival as a new member of Parliament. Speeches were made and about an hour into the meeting delegates were given a chance to ask questions. A male stood up, and with uncertainty as to if he was about to cry, he said in a wailing voice, "How can we convince people that we are not evil? I have ineffectively tried to explain to family and friends that we simply want to save the welfare state." In this instance I thought to myself that this is the perfect example of how effective the left wing's emotional terrorism is, and how forcefully collectivist narcissistic coercion can subdue the individual self.

Truly ironic is when asking a collectivist if a person with low self-esteem or someone who has been brainwashed would be aware of being in those states. The instantaneous compulsive answer—with almost no exceptions—always is "yes!" I have therefore on several occasions—for research purposes—intentionally pushed these exact buttons, triggering the collectivist's impulses to act defensively upon their feelings of severe inferiority. Proving them instantly wrong by writing down the exact outcome—words, reactions, and even sentences—prior to the discussion and thereby proving the ability to predict their exact reactions. However, even with proof sitting right there in front of them—again not wanting to expose their ignorance—through personal illusion (magical thinking), they will completely deny acting subconsciously on behalf of these inhibitions.

Confronting collectivists with facts is one way to obstruct their magical thinking. To get them to admit anything contrary to the collective thought is no different than getting any justice system to admit misconduct: one gets nowhere. Confrontations only provoke collectivists to act defensively upon their deprived narcissistic emotions.

The collectivists' techniques of manipulation can be predicted in detail, as can their reactions. Although collectivists are truly elusive, with the right insight one can easily corner them; their reactions are so predictable that a debate can be scripted beforehand.

PREDICTING A DEBATE

When confronted with reality, textbook left-wing collectivists show typical signs:

(1) Compulsive denial, often followed by projections or by diverting attention to another subject. This is caused by magical thinking and, therefore, is generally mounted with an arrogant attitude and haughty behavior. Females often turn toward expressing self-importance. Without any actual insight or knowledge, they are still absolutely convinced they know the truth. Without any intent of learning or listening, they always know better. This quite quickly proves their arrogant ignorance (magical thinking), and therefore, their absolutely deprived omniscient mindset.

(2) The weapon of guilt is now used to coerce—attempted dominance is often achieved through manipulation or reverse psychology—with frequent blame externalization and projections of moral superiority by dumping shame. Nonetheless, since the collectivist thrives in ignorance, one should always challenge their knowledge. Ask and demand they define their previously used terms or subjects as well as their frequently used condemnations. Always demand straight yes or no answers. This will aggravate them and again lead to denial, often switching to another subject, in combination with infinite excuses, "buts" and "ifs," and oftentimes, intimidation, name-calling, and even aggression. If a narcissistic injury has not occurred by now, the collectivist is either a female or the person's level of pathological narcissism is likely moderate; however, pushing the debate much further will result in narcissistic injury.

(3) Collectivists live in a grandiose fantasy world of superficial sympathy. As a result of subconscious self-pity, they believe themselves to be motivated by caring for the welfare of others. In addition, there are the usual reverse psychological catchphrases (e.g., "How can anyone be insinuating that my wanting to help people in any way makes me selfish?"). Behind this message of altruism, the magical illusion of unity and selflessness, is always the collectivist's factual egocentric agenda, or what they personally acquire from collectivism. Therefore, always direct the collectivist back to the true subject: their own personal needs. My usual argument against collectivist statements is to say, "If you want to help others, then vote for fewer taxes and give away what is rightfully yours: your own time and money that you do not need." But then again, that is not what the collectivist wants, because this form or action demands responsibility, ambition, and the risk of failure.

(4) Their narcissistic egos are exposed and feeling cornered—this being the resultant narcissistic injury, or clear signs of bad boundaries (entitlement)—creating the pathological delusion that you, the perpetrator, are an awkward or difficult person. Hence, the collectivist now generally resorts to leaving the premises, usually mounted by condemnations, in some way implementing the weapon of guilt, and in the process, generally applying anger and attitude, including attitudinal body language, aggression, and name-calling. They will likely never talk to you again. However, as the victor of the debate, all you can do is to sit back and wait for the storm. Setting up people against one another is their absolute area of expertise. They will never back down.

Quick tools to easily spot a collectivist and the signs of pathological narcissism:

- Draws quick conclusions without any insight knowledge
- Uses projection and name-calling; attempts to force shame upon others
- Always knows better
- Always blames others
- Compulsively judgmental and opinionated
- Impulsively corrects, polices, and tries to control their surroundings
- Lacks the ability to take criticism
- Expects absolute compliance with their ways, views, and ideas
- Goes from friendly to fiercely hostile in only seconds, and then behaves calmly a split second later
- Unwilling or unable to distinguish between themselves and others
- Talks in plural ("we"); speaks on behalf of others and society
- Remains elusive; likely never gives straight yes or no answers
- Feels aggravated by the lack of reciprocal affirmation for their appreciation in others
- Fails to accept responsibility for personal actions
- Believes that others are, and should be, treated entirely as equals to them without mandatory achievement. Compatible behavior is expecting to be recognized as superior to others without mandatory achievements (superiority complex)

Subconscious fears and feelings of inadequacy and exposure in perfect combination with the lack of ability to be self-critical—caused by feeling perfect—generally cause defensive contempt for any therapeutic processes; a great indicator of pathological narcissism is, therefore, quite simply denial that psychology is beneficial.

Psychology provides truly powerful tools that rarely lie, and thus act as the strongest weapon against collectivism, of which a war of words must be fought.

"You must be the change you wish to see in the world."
—MAHATMA GANDHI

A PERSONAL SOCIAL EXPERIMENT

One of the easiest ways to prove how predictable collectivists truly are is with the social experiment that follows: When shopping at the supermarket, after having placed the groceries on the checkout conveyor belt, experiment with the simple act of not placing down the checkout divider, the gadget that one uses to distinguish one's groceries from the next customer's.

With almost no exceptions, this failure to act in accordance with subliminal rules will set off the collectivist's excessive sense of entitlement and will frequently result in irritation, argumentation, projections, and oftentimes name-calling. The experiment is a perfect example of deception that drives collectivists to believe that they are given a personal choice in democratic socialism. The illusion of selflessness and the concern for the welfare of others are but co-dependent measures to avoid feeling personal guilt.

This example works perfectly in a radicalized collectivist society, thus the recommendation is for this social experiment to be attempted more than once. More cultural freedoms and individual choice can be measured in the accruing narcissistic behaviors; hence, falsely perceived by collectivists as social norms, these are brought forth in this social experiment.

Please don't fool yourself, as here the collectivist again alters reality. The following example has absolutely nothing to do with common courtesy as you can assure yourself that the next person in the checkout line, in one way or another with the intent to create guilt, will show signs of disapproval or utter their dissatisfaction. In reality, these principles are decided by the collective human organism. Triggered by co-dependency, more or less all collectivists will automatically obtain immediate guilt if they don't place down this divider.

Truly unique is the collectivist's amazing ability to show disapproval without actually using any words. As mentioned previously, passive coercion is often accomplished in public simply by staring. This undermining collectivist technique, one that is truly effective on the frail mind, is applied in various ways in an attempt to create guilt.

In the example above—the checkout divider social experiment—disapproval is often made known with a silent statement of calmly squashing or pushing oneself past the person who did not place the checkout divider or by banging it down as one roughly places the divider or the groceries on the conveyor belt.

When a person in the queue before me kindly places the divider for me, I always thank them. In response, they do not generally turn toward me to acknowledge my kind comment. If they turn toward me, often they instead look at me with absolute amazement or contempt. Driven by a strong sense of entitlement, of course they take this seemingly curious gesture for granted.

Though the true question to ask in this social experiment would be this: can anything be about common courtesy—like the altruistic illusion of selflessness that is perceived in collectivism as voluntary—when the individual's right to personally determine if one wants to show a kind gesture is actually predetermined? That is, predetermined by the fact that an inaction as simple as this can trigger people to go noticeably mental. Actions of common courtesy are not truly actions of a kind gesture but are actually measures of expectation applied to avoid confrontations or feelings of personal guilt; therefore, in reality, they are actions of co-dependency and are not truly kind gestures at all.

"Don't become a mere recorder of facts, but try to penetrate the mystery of their origin."
—IVAN PAVLOV

CHAPTER NINE

AMBIENT SOCIALISM

The word "social" in socialism is completely deceptive regarding the word's true meaning. "Social" is a word which most are persuaded to think defines communal, together, or sharing. But no, a socialist is but a communist in disguise. The word social in socialism, in reality only defines communism's attempt to compete with capitalism's free market by seemingly allowing "social class defenses." Yet, there is a fierce rejection of even mentioning class difference in democratic socialism, and further, by seemingly allowing ownership of personal property. Caused and controlled by extreme tax levels, you will never truly own anything.

Denmark, a nation without a political right wing, has achieved neo-communism. What Danes deceitfully refer to as a welfare or socialistic democracy—to deceive people from the truth—is but another attempt to repeat what has been tried too many times before, having previously failed. History suggests that Marxism could work on a voluntary basis in a smaller community, yet it can never work as a society.

Socialism democratically commences as liberty, next as collectivism, disguised as modern liberalism—deceitfully using the term liberal—then as socialist, and so forth. The goal is to deprive societies' citizenry emotionally, thereby creating co-dependency, and so subliminally moving each and every political party to the left wing of the political scale, effectively achieving neo-communism.

Socialism can be summed up as the redistribution of wealth to create social equality by taking from the ones who are more successful and distributing it to all—in the name of placating envy. This lies in contrast to welfare, whose goal is to provide basic needs only for humanity's "absolute" weakest. Apart from Marxism's seemingly democratic process, Denmark's lifestyle has essentially the same structure and aspects as actual communism. The difference between society being owned by everyone, which is communism, and Denmark's neo-communism is that the government completely controls society with legalized political corruption from outrageous taxation, of which large tax burdens generally remain purposely hidden. Though no democracy can ever justify stealing, outrageous taxation makes this possible. Along with this is the complete exploitation of the general citizenry's inability to leave the country because of nationalistic feelings and family relations.

Socialist politics are established on the basis that "all are and should be treated equally." These are all self-loving principles—severe pathological narcissism and hypocrisy at its absolute best. They gladly discriminate by supporting a higher income tax for the more prosperous citizenry, what many have come to refer to as envy tax. Thus, socialist democrats and farther right collectivists have cunningly outwitted other socialist parties by twisting these Marxist principles to "all should have equal opportunities."

In search of a scapegoat, Marxism's constant tyrannical and damaging emotional terrorism drives Marxists to turn their feelings of inferiority, hurt, and anger into envy by punishing people who are more successful. Whereas in the case of national-socialists, this need for blame extermination, fascists in general find their scapegoats in other races, groups, or nationalities.

Severe pathological narcissism creates envy and the urge to feel equal, and the punishment is a massive support of envy taxes. This again hurts the natural source, the reward for self-motivation and innovation amongst people who would otherwise have reached higher goals. The economic subordination commences.

The problem with envy taxes, and taxes in general, can be compared to playing the lottery. People gamble, in pursuit of happiness, taking a chance in hopes of hitting the jackpot. Conversely, the less money there is to gamble, and the higher the reward is taxed, the less people care to gamble. Envy tax is the thin gap between engaging in socialism and living in liberty. Envy taxation is the worst mistake society can ever make, as it is a suppressive tool with one purpose only: allowing Marxists to subordinate society by destroying the more prosperous citizenry, in addition to spoiling personal willingness to strive for a more prosperous life. The assured result is stagnation (i.e., economic distrust, lack of investments, businesses moved abroad, and outsourcing) and economic oppression resulting in massive losses of employment. This economic subordination of society will, however, sooner rather than later deceitfully be referred to as "welfare."

In Denmark, the envy tax increases to 68 percent if one makes more than 80,000 U.S. dollars annually, which is supported by all but one political party in Denmark—the farthest right center-left wing. The tax rate for the lowest income level starts in the range of 37–42 percent. All citizens in Denmark are afforded tax-relief on annual incomes below 8,000 U.S. dollars. Thus, with the extreme high cost of living caused by a sales tax of 25 percent, on top of further generally hidden duties and fees applied to almost everything, the government levies on average easily reach 80 percent, even for the lower income household in Denmark.

Keeping people apathetic with severe pathological narcissism is indeed crucial to the collectivist pathological mind-game. In fact, this is evident when Danes are asked how much levies from their earnings are returned to the government by people who are residing in Denmark permanently. Ignorant as most collectivists are, a majority answers "around 40 percent!" Hence, should people start to question reality, this scheme would completely fall apart. In truth, having already reached advanced tax-burdens, the government is likely never to raise obvious taxes—those taxes taken directly by the government (e.g., paychecks, tax returns). Rather, the government cunningly sneaks upon society through increases in duties and fees since these generally go unnoticed.

In this exact part of the collectivist pathological mind game, feminism plays an ever so important role. While feminism can be seen from a positive perspective, having liberated women from certain conservative norms and gotten women into the workforce, in reality this is a necessary step for governments to achieve exceedingly high tax burdens. Indeed, feminism has seemingly made women freer. The truth, however, is awful and extremely obscured. In fact, with the excessive government tax burdens in Denmark, the average household actually cannot manage a standard middle-class living without two working parents. Consequently, and similar to communism where children are brought up by society, in Denmark's neo-communism only a few children are ever truly raised by their parents. This in turn disrupts the family ties, thus perfectly shifting the balance from reliance on the family to dependence on Big Mother Denmark, the government.

In truth, collectivists envy the prosperous lifestyle. Thus, with excessively high tax burdens, and to achieve a middle-class standard of living, Danes are forced to turn to banks. Consequently, making democratic socialism into humanity's most perfect and obscured form of slavery, bank-slavery. Fact is, Denmark is built purely on Marxism's "planned-economy." Danes haven't seen the shadow of any genuine capitalism (free-market/free-trade) or experienced freedom from non-intrusive government for numerous decades. According to (*Organization for Economic Co-operation and Development* data), Denmark factually holds the highest household debt in the western world as a percentage of gross disposable income. Actually, private household debt in Denmark exceeds the United States by more than double. Consequently, while bankers worldwide assumedly are laughing and clapping their hands over this system, Danes have made themselves into slaves, not only to their own emotions but to lifelong personal debts as well. Danes are slaves to the exact same elite, bankers and monetary system—in their ignorant view, the capitalist system—that collectivists loathe.

Metaphorically speaking, society can be compared to a loaf of bread, representing the more prosperous citizenry. The bigger the loaf, the more slices—representing innovation and vital investments it creates—and for each slice, bread crumbs will drop—representing jobs created. One can never successfully build a nation on punishment for contributing. Indeed, citizens should reward achievements to assure an increase in personal endeavor—the pursuit of happiness.

Envy tax brings in short-term revenue, but as the ladder of self-motivation and more prosperous citizenry is subordinated, the actual losses of employment positions, and for the same reason state tax revenue, are a great deal higher. Some are fortunate enough to be born into wealth; however, one should never forget that regardless how small the percentage paid in tax, the wealthy populace still provides the largest economic contribution to the general public. On top, the wealthy frequently have gone through truly difficult times and taken chances gambling with their personal assets and time—with the risk of losing all their personal assets—to achieve as much as they have. Sooner or later they create the most important contribution—the most any nation can ever ask for—which is not tax money, but the creation of employment.

AN EVERYDAY STORY

A perfect example of collectivism's assimilation occurred shortly after my family and I moved back to Denmark from Australia. I remember that it happened one night when watching a live comedy show on television. Suddenly my wife cried out, "Look, Danes are communists; they even clap as one!" She was right, the crowd clapped completely synchronized—something I had often seen—yet never thought about before.

It all starts with the weapon of guilt—allowing socialism's average tax increase to nanny societies' poorest—this increases the cost of living, and will, assuredly, lead to demands for higher salaries. This is, however, to the government's advantage, as it achieves its intended goal: government dependency. All this is for the benefit of government, as it destroys competitiveness for both private businesses and industry and thereby creates recession.

Keynesian economics slowly and simultaneously makes its impact during this societal subordination. Independent workers with jobs in the private sector have now been replaced by dependency on government benefits and government jobs. This cycle of state favoritism will continue growing the government as taxes increase and demands for ever higher salaries persist.

Free-market capitalism is slowly destroyed by the government's bureaucratic interference. In time it will be replaced with the government's planned economy. Private businesses and industry will eventually shrink to such extremes that the government will need to find money elsewhere. With the prosperous citizenry already overly taxed, the government turns to the middle-class pocket through increases in personal tax and higher, generally hidden sales taxes, duties, and fees. This once again creates demands for higher salaries. Eventually living expenses rise to extreme levels, two to three times above average. Taxes and expenses by no means make up for losses from unemployment and the small return of socialism's entitlement benefits. Free-market capitalism is replaced with a system of blackmail, tax slavery, and financial oppression, all now cunningly portrayed as welfare.

In this progressive subordination, generally hidden taxes, duties, and fees are applied to everything, including groceries and clothing, which hypocritically is harder on the average middle and lower-class citizenry, not the few aristocrats left in the nation or the upper middle-class citizens.

Recently I went to Burger King and ordered a large milkshake and a Whopper, which with the added taxes and high salaries, consequently cost me about 15 U.S. dollars. The assured result of high taxation of basic goods is government dependency, which is of course to the government's benefit.

Fact is, the world's biggest shipping company, Mearsk Sealand, is the only reason Denmark seems prosperous. Without this company, Denmark's lifestyle would literally be no higher than any of the East European countries. The company contributes annual commercial taxes of approximately 7 billion US dollars, which is over half of Denmark's commercial taxes in total.

One could be persuaded to think that socialism helps the poorest and gives the middle class more; unfortunately, the truth is quite the opposite. It is absolutely correct that Marxism redistributes wealth; however, when Marxism has destroyed the upper class and results in a depressed economy, there is much less money to redistribute. When the upper class is destroyed, so is the wealth and necessary investments that create jobs; with this comes the subordination of the prosperous middle class. The middle class then bears the burden of the ever more demanding lower class—a process that slowly subordinates the middle class—eventually creating an equilibrated lower-middle class.

One problem of many with democratic socialism is that it spoils the weakest, through both indulgence and deprivation, thereby discouraging personal effort. People simply stop caring about reaching higher limits. With the social ladder eliminated, this is the case even with behavioral self-improvement, the reason for the reward of accomplishment is corrupted; consequently, people are disabled from understanding higher values since they never have been nor will be truly tested. The natural chain of self-motivation and innovation (incentive) is immobilized, and the populace is weakened. The certain result is an enormously deprived lower-middle class who constantly demands more be given to it, rather than giving to others. Slowly, the nation reaches stagnation.

A majority of society's citizenry will eventually go as far as to speculate if one actually cares to find employment or if one should exploit the government benefits. And just as society's citizenry will exploit the entitlement system—with its inviting big fat nanny advertisement—so will immigrants naturally do anything to utilize the immigration system to get a piece of it.

The truly disruptive part is that government bureaucracy purposely makes it difficult to build a business. Irrefutable proof affirms that business ownership leads people toward liberating themselves. Once the average collectivist's life situation changes, self-esteem begins to increase. The person can now take better care of themselves and first tries to pay high taxes, then the collectivist gradually begins voting for farther right political parties. Collectivists generally have no problem voting for political parties that support higher taxes, but no one queries working for money under the table. Both examples prove the collectivist's hypocrisy and lack of empathy. Collectivists are prepared to exploit others for personal gain and willingly do to others what they would not want others to do to them.

Everything in neo-communism is under government control—no bank account or pharmaceutical purchase is private. In truth, there is nothing in Denmark over which Big Brother is not in complete control. The Danes are the world's highest taxed people; the infrastructure is completely monopolized, corrupted by state favoritism. The government is in fact the country's biggest employer, in direct competition with private businesses and industry. Similar to communism, in the neo-communist system almost everything is owned by the government—this includes administration of employment services and postal services; transportation including aviation and airports, buses, subways, and railways; and public services such as communications and power plants. In addition, the government has control through its oversight of education, or government indoctrination centers: daycare, schools, and universities. Moreover, many are dependent on public housing. Getting into a government apartment project generally takes under five years in rural areas, yet placement can take up to twenty-five years in the denser populated cities. The state even owns television and radio stations, corner stores, and hotels—controversially, caused by governmental favoritism, these hotels are the two tallest buildings in the country. The assuring result is even further governmental favoritism since people rely upon jobs in the government for their livelihood. The title government official practically works as a status equivalent to communist party members in China or the former Soviet Union. These egomaniacs are untouchable as they are never found at fault, regardless. This protected status is applied to anyone working within the government.

So no one can indulge themselves more than others, the envy tax on a car is 180 percent—which easily brings a car valued a bit over 20,000 U.S. dollars (e.g., Honda Accord) in the United States close to an astounding 50,000 U.S. dollars in Denmark. This is not to mention that the average cost of achieving a driver's license is close to 2,500 U.S. dollars. Almost no one owns a new car in Denmark—banks generally do. Once again, hypocritically, the very same bankers that the collectivists despise. So the majority ride bicycles, drive a secondhand wreck, or utilize the triple-overpriced public transportation. And now that green is the newest trend, reasons as to why to ride a bicycle give them yet another excuse to make up their pathological lies.

The same result is achieved in Denmark's neo-communism as is in a country where communism has been accomplished by an obvious and direct fascist military takeover; in all cases, one is given just about whatever one needs. Excessively high salaries—Denmark's being among the world's highest—creates imaginary prosperity. Even after an average low-income tax of around 40 percent, one seems prosperous. The bliss though is short lived as the deceptive part is hidden in the triple-overpriced living expenses (the result of the extremely high service cost caused by these tremendously high salaries), and the overall cost of living is so high that an average hardworking middle-class citizen rarely dines out. Finding revenue for a decent vacation is not something one does with ease. Nor is covering the dentist bill and day-care, which are the only entitlement benefits that are not completely free of personal charge "yet," unless one receives welfare. This struggle to afford simple "luxuries," in turn, assures the perfect environment for continual envy.

The ignorance of democratic socialism is, however, only bliss for as long as the maligned narcissistic tyranny balances out itself with the blinding tools of fictive contentment, found in the government's bribery with entitlement benefits. Margaret Thatcher, aka the Iron Lady, once said, "The problem with socialism is that you eventually run out of other people's money," which is exactly the point in time when government addicts—mandates in need of their daily fix of adulation, attention, or affirmation (narcissistic supply)—and so addicted to gambling for other people's money—start making up for the lack of funding by taking out loans to nurture the lower-middle class's ever increasing demand for more, and thereby attain their necessary fix of admiration by vote.

"Gambling problem," also known in technical terms as "ludomania," is the urge to continuously gamble despite harmful negative consequences. Hence, the political acts of a corrupt collectivist syndicate that exploits the authority invested in the power of democracy, thus infiltrating the government for the purpose of blackmailing its fellow citizens, is no more a "democracy." A society controlled by a government, empowering itself through blackmail and bribery, gambling for votes with stolen private assets, is more appropriately referred to as a "ludomocracy."

For the liberated observer, only now does the truly amusing part begin. The government is now in need of make-believe and will, therefore, devise any excuse to defer and manipulate its citizenry in order to persuade them that higher taxes, duties, and fees are absolutely necessary. This is, however, no problem, as society has now achieved a totalitarian state. These deprived ignorant citizens—weakened by severe pathological narcissism—are living in a fantasy world. They are in awe of authority, convinced that the government takes care of them (because the dog never bites the hand that feeds it); therefore, they don't question or criticize society or society's structure, unless of course something is to be taken away from them.

Controversially, the argument every time for raising taxes, duties, and fees is: "The government knows best, and you, the citizenry, can't think for yourselves. Your government will, therefore, have to take away your rights of personal choice and raise taxes, duties, and fees on items (e.g., tanning services, soda pop, fattening products), as they are unhealthy." Marxist parties will never decrease taxes. They might state their intent to do so, but being the manipulative pathological liars they are, they will only give some in one place while taking from somewhere else.

Debates began in 2011 around a politician's living example of a poor person in Denmark with the pseudonym "poor Carina." Her story epitomizes learned helplessness (excessive entitlement), being the story of a thirty-six year old mother of two on welfare since she was sixteen. Carina had received cash and benefits (e.g., free daycare, education, medicine) reaching in the proximity of 500,000 U.S. dollars. Carina's personal claim was that she was so poor that she could not afford a cinema ticket for her child on her monthly government benefit of around 3,000 U.S. dollars after tax. However, when the debating politicians entered her decent apartment, it was discovered that she had an upstanding living arrangement with nice furniture and a flat-screen TV, not to mention that she was able to maintain her 500 kroner (100 USD) per month smoking habit. Her case is just one amongst tens of thousands. Let us not forget the abundance of substance addicts and alcoholics whose addiction is in fact sponsored by the taxpayer—again government bribery (money for misery), with absolutely no intent to solve the actual true origin of the matter. The reason Carina gave as for being unable to afford a cinema ticket was that she had just bought a brand new sofa for 900 U.S. dollars.

Entitlement benefits (e.g., social security and other similar entitlements) being taxed in ways identical to capital income and genuine earned income allows yet another illusion among collectivists. The ideal illusive argument (for the deprived mind) is that the recipient pays tax like any other citizen; consequently, this allows the perfect excuse for taking part in the democratic process and being entitled to benefits since one is a contributor to society.

Rhetorically one asks, how in fact can people who are not contributing to society, who are obviously not competent enough to make educated decisions in their own lives and for that reason on behalf of society, still be given the responsibility of taking part in the democratic process? How can these people who have proven themselves incompetent have the right to dig the grave for all of society, by voting themselves handouts of other people's money? Stories such as poor Carina's are the strongest evidence to support the case that a person should be able to vote only for as long as one contributes to society. Being part of the voting process should be a reward and pledged as an honor.

The essence to a democracy is in fact "complete government transparency." However, Denmark has already passed laws keeping Denmark's citizenry from inside knowledge into the movements of government mandates. Additionally, in Denmark anyone can vote without a valid picture ID. Consequently, electoral rigging is a fact. Thus, with government transparency gone and voter fraud unrestrained, Denmark has long ago proven itself a tyranny.

Socialism, democratically, is calculated tax-slavery. To this day it stands as the smartest and most obscured form of political corruption on record—justified blackmail by abusing the power of democracy—a society slowly eating itself by the tail.

"Democracy is the road to socialism."
—KARl MARX

CHAPTER TEN

BIG MOTHER'S INDOCTRINATION PROGRAM

Starting from birth, the menu of free-of-charge luxury goodies—entitlement benefits most people in the world have never dreamt of, or ever heard about—are almost unlimited in Denmark. It is therefore easier to mention the only two that are not free of personal charge "yet": dental care—though free of personal charge until the age of eighteen—and daycare, which based on family income, starts at just under 400 U.S. dollars, though it is free of personal charge while collecting social security or student funding. Yes you read correctly—in Denmark one is paid to study, and education is free of personal charge all the way up to and including university. Education free of personal charge is counted as one of the government's most vital entitlement programs. Education at all levels acts as a government indoctrination program, there to purchase votes, in order to perpetuate democratic socialism.

Students generally view student funding as a salary for studying. Hence, when students are confronted with the fact that viewing student funding as a wage should then equally allow the same requirements as a normal job by cutting this so called wage to penalize for absence from classes, the entitlement and infinite excuses are again at display.

Since the educational system in Denmark became free of personal charge in the late-middle twentieth century (the social bullies have become highly influential in academics with the habituation of this now common narcissistic mentality in the general population), the last right-wing conservatives and classical liberals (libertarians) have steadily become, subdued, radicalized, and assimilated over the last forty years into Marxism's collective human organism.

MACHIAVELLIAN EGOCENTRICITY

The true dawn of collectivism in the United States, and a great example of collectivism's bad boundaries, manipulative techniques, and envy, became truly evident in April 2000 when the Danish drummer Lars Ulrich from the famous heavy metal band Metallica took legal action against the website Napster.com after Metallica's entire catalogue was found to be freely available for download on Napster's online service. Metallica, consequently, filed a lawsuit against the company for copyright infringement and racketeering. The case was settled out of court, resulting in more than 300,000 Napster users being banned from the website.

Lars Ulrich was the focal point of the backlash that became the perfect example of the force of collectivist manipulation techniques. This coercion is difficult to recognize if one is not aware of exactly what to look for. If one searches the Internet on sites such as YouTube for stories about the case, one will find numerous disdainful videos mocking Metallica. All with the same irrational argument of scornful envy, "You have so much and are greedy, so it justifies us stealing from you!" This is ambient abuse (Machiavellian egocentricity) with one intent only: to attain dominance by utilizing the weapon of guilt. So which is worse I ask, "Expecting to get things for free, stealing, and claiming the right to someone else's possessions," or "Wanting to keep one's hard-earned assets and other personal possessions"? Greedy or not, the argument is powerful reverse psychology—manipulative techniques largely used by narcissists—coercion so powerful that it not only eventually had Lars Ulrich apologizing, but literally had him apologizing for opposing practices that stole what was rightfully his.

The urge to control others and the need for full compliance (never to be contradicted, confronted, or disapproved of) leads narcissists to seek out superior mind-controlling positions. Not many places of employment provide a more soothing environment for the maladaptive collectivist narcissist's inferiority complexes than the institutions of education, where the collectivist mind has control of the subservient child or adolescent. Known in Denmark as pedagogues, child-caregivers and teachers are with almost no exceptions fascists, socialists and communists. Pedagogy, which means to lead the child, is a perfect construct of teaching ideals used by Marxists—built on theories, amongst others, such as liberating children from their parents at an early age. These theories of social education and social inclusion entirely disguise Marxism's intended agenda, which is to convert the child's individual identity into a collective ego. This necessary programming of bad boundaries is easily achieved, considering the deprived collectivist-parent's abdication of responsibility. The child is released into the total control and care of society and government through these pedagogic caregivers' and teachers' complete upbringing of the child.

The truly awful part in this mind game, and the part that no Marxist wants you to know, is that the daycare and public school system—the governmental indoctrination program—is where the personality mind control of manipulism is progressively implemented. It is a slow, subliminal process of correctional lectures—forming adaptation to the Marxist's maladaptive behavior—gradually increasing with age. The pedagogue initially endeavors to persuade the child of the unimportance of expressing self-assurance or self-encouragement; rather, to fit in, to follow suit, is of the utmost importance. The coercion then intensifies dramatically during the years of adolescence. Perfectly assessed by society's maligned narcissistic tyranny—a denial of the emerging individual self—the assuring result is severe inferiority complex, therefore, necessitating co-dependency, and the successful radicalization of even the most liberated child.

In countries like these, the governmental Big Brother (bad boundaries) is everywhere—like a fly on the wall. Authorities' power comes from laws intruding into an area more private than the four walls of one's own home, in fact with laws that reach into one's mind. Not that I particularly believe in alcohol consumption around children, but it is out of the question to simply socialize over a beer after work with your coworkers if the next step in your daily routine is to pick up your children from daycare. Any hint of your having consumed alcohol gives these child-caregivers authority not to hand over your children. Pedagogue child-caregivers and teachers—any entitled government official in general—will go through walls to attempt to set up the system against anyone who would challenge their abilities, including denying, manipulating, and intimidating any perpetrator opposing their authority. These child-caregivers, hired as governmental watchdogs, keep a constant eye on parents' movements. They watch for something as simple as not having a stable routine or wanting to keep the child at home for the day instead of in daycare. No privacy exists in this Big Bother society, and desire for privacy can even be perceived as a sign of trouble in the family.

Childhood in democratic socialism is completely effortless, the spoiled life, like that of a child born into extreme wealth. Children spoiled by the deprived collectivist-parent's utter lack of challenges will display dependency on the system and a lack of endeavor. The first few years of adolescence are a critical period, when self-reliance or dependency will be determined. Depending upon the severity of their pathological narcissism, young adults may still likely remain open to enlightenment, although the youths are generally already driven by severe inferiority complexes. Marxist parties, preying on ignorance with guilt and bribery, purchase a great percentage of votes from first-time voters—exploitative parasites that neither care about, nor are experienced in, politics—and young people who are receiving an education. In fact the government's preferred voter is one who says, "I do not care for politics," yet still chooses to vote.

Quite frankly, that taxes would be better used on what Marxists always frame as the hallmark of their motivation—to care for the weakest. My childhood friend who was abused sexually for years by his stepfather was offered no help by the government, as often, disadvantaged people are neglected for Marxism's greed. Luxury benefits, established to bring about social equilibration, in no way benefit the weakest. The quarterly child-benefits check that all parents—both rich and poor—in Denmark receive (even the queen) is as high as 1,500 dollars.

A Marxist is not very different from a rich man's spoiled child. Give Marxists a hand and the ever-increasing public entitlement will assure they eventually demand your whole arm—enough is never enough. With the escalating entitlement, learned helplessness assures the monetary lower class's ever-increasing demand for more entitlement benefits. It never stops; thus, Marxists will do anything to persuade otherwise. It all starts with food coupons that eventually become actual cash in hand—social security benefits will eventually be as high as in Denmark, where security benefits can be as high as an ordinary factory worker's income of 3,000 dollars after taxes. Next comes universal health care, and so, progressively, Marxists move on to education. In Denmark, everyone receives education free of personal charge. In addition, students receive funding of more than 1,500 dollars monthly if they are raising a child, with an additional benefit of two to three months on average of annual government-funded holiday. Furthermore, students have the option of taking out governmental-provided monthly loans of around 800 dollars, and students still living at home with their parents can receive more than 400 dollars monthly. This provides the perfect means for bribing adolescents at an early age to favor Mother Denmark, the government's far-left left wing.

This money literally goes to personal indulgence. When young students are asked why society should support them rather than requiring them to get a part-time job while being supported (living in their parents' home), my research showed that these students immediately would cite their need for personal luxuries such as mobile phone use, party lifestyles, and smoking habits.

What else is provided free of personal charge? Trees for the garden, personal computers, and work sabbaticals. And as mentioned earlier, holidays, breast implants, artificial impregnation, and the list goes on and on. This points toward one among many of Marxism's major problems: greed. In general, Marxists think of money as the solution to society's problems. All this is bribery to ensure equilibrium, when better solutions can be found by focusing on society's problems on an emotional level.

One cannot avoid thinking: "No, money does not grow on trees." Hypocritically, the most commonly employed Marxist techniques of compulsive projections are "Liberals are greedy," or "Liberals only think about themselves." Deprived as they are, Marxists feel that people who want to keep their own money are greedy, yet humorously, the Marxists do not consider themselves greedy for feeling entitled to other people's money. Deceitfully, these projections of guilt are forced upon left-wing collectivists, center-left–wing social liberals on Denmark's imaginary right wing.

NOT AN EVERYDAY STORY

In the process of writing this book, I resided in a low-income apartment complex. During my daily routine to pick up my children from school, I regularly observed a young woman in her early to mid-twenties waiting at the bus stop. This young woman simply shined with a sense of kindness about her, always passing the biggest smile. Being quite out of character, in no way fitting the behavior of the average Dane, therefore, the thought had shamefully crossed my mind as to if she were sane. Summer had arrived, and one day I arrived at the bus stop early. She arrived and as always passed the kindest smile. Although it is not common to talk to strangers, I impulsively asked in Danish, "Where do you get all the joy from? You always smile so nicely." "Sorry, I don't understand Danish," the girl replied with an American English accent. I instantly cried out in English, "Oh, now I understand perfectly."

In my years of observation and research, I did find one good thing about Marxism: socialism's freely available resources of luxury benefits can be utilized against itself. In order to complete this book, for years now I have spent all the money I have ever saved as well as using the free funding and education system in order to attend lectures, seminars, and courses. The education has made it possible for me to observe and analyze behavior, and thereby to verify and finalize my theories as well as to correct flaws in my research on Marxist mentality. Most importantly, it allowed me to write and thoroughly infiltrate the educational system and research its methods of indoctrination.

If one knows what to look for, Marxism's ways of indoctrination (i.e., prejudices, condemnation, and scornful envy) can be found everywhere and in everything in Denmark. This extends into all areas including educational material, advertisements, pamphlets, TV shows, and music—even kids' songs. For that exact reason, I undertook a whole semester, a college social science class, to observe behavior and teaching methods. Throughout the course, I kept one question in mind:

how can highly educated people be kept from, or keep themselves from, realizing reality? The experience was astounding. I can say with 100 percent certainty that not one of the participating undergraduates in the course of a whole year's education ever moved an inch politically. Marxism's propaganda, "Liberalism; humanity is egotistical," was emphasized throughout the learning material and elaborated on verbally numerous times throughout the course of the year. Studies were based more on learning terminology—to sound educated—than on studying and analyzing social science fact.

Economist Milton Friedman, the Nobel Prize recipient, was mentioned (once by name) during the year-long course, but Marxism's preferred economist, John Maynard Keynes, was the name of the game. Classical liberalism/libertarianism was never mentioned.

The invention of a right wing on the collectivist left wing surpasses any other attempted deception in Marxism's pathological indoctrination scheme, perfectly enabling ignorance and deception such as portraying the national socialist Adolf Hitler as a right-winger. Thus, Marxism's tools of deception are often hidden in obvious facts entirely and intentionally avoided.

The government's choice of educational material is among the best examples of the government's deception. The complete government-controlled curriculum included statistic booklets on practically all subjects, except statistics on suicide and depression. Or better stated, information could be found on anything except what is critical of socialism.

Statistics in regard to homelessness, however, proved to be some of the most purposely misleading. Only one nation was ever compared to Denmark's homelessness rate: the United States, of course. Bear in mind that Marxists, driven by severe inferiority complex, dread the confident individualistic American. None of the numerous nations in Europe, such as Austria, Italy, or Switzerland—

all with lower homelessness rates than Denmark's—were ever mentioned.

I once observed the teacher conferring with a student, with pride and excitement, about how the university she had attended openly indoctrinated academic delegates into supporting a specific radicalized socialist party. Indoctrination succeeded in making this teacher elusive; regardless of how much I intentionally provoked her with controversial questions, she would simply defer to another subject, attempt to set up the class against me, seem uninterested in my comments, or disregard my questions.

During this class, Russia, the end result of communism, was never mentioned. With an estimated 143.4 million residents, an estimated 5 million Russian people are homeless (approximately 3.5 percent of the population), whereof 1 million are estimated to be children. Neither was there mention of the neo-communist nation of France, the near-end result of democratic socialism. France, with an estimated 60 million residents and skyrocketing taxes, recently raised its tax levels to as high as 75 percent. France's homelessness rate, estimated to be around 1 million people (approximately 1.6 percent of the population), is at least double that of the United States. In America, with an estimated population of 310 million people, the United States homeless guesstimates range from as low as 600,000 to as high as 2,500,000 (approximately 0.2 to 0.8 percent of the population). The statistics for the European Union with around 500 million people, estimate 3 million people to be homeless (approximately 0.6 percent of the population). Compare these statistics to Denmark, with an estimated population of 5.5 million people and where homelessness is estimated to be 10,000–12,000 (approximately 0.2 percent of the population).

These are just a few of the many examples in Denmark of "socialism is the best" propaganda, the perfect pathological mind game. The government's attempt to indoctrinate using an ideal cocktail of bribery, a lifetime of societal coercion, an education free of personal charge, perfectly disables any source of skepticism, questionability, or criticism toward authorities or society's structure.

"Freedom is never more than one generation away from extinction. We didn't pass it to our children in the bloodstream. It must be fought for, protected, and handed on for them to do the same."
—RONALD REAGAN

AFTERWORD

Regardless where one is situated in the world, contentment is an absolute universal need. This need finds its highest satisfaction when contentment is found within. Contentment need not be influenced by one's surroundings or anything fictive. Pure contentment comes from no outside source whatsoever, but simply is found within. Therefore, as the author of this book, I cannot avoid a grin on my face when stating that one is only truly content when one feels no need to convince others.

Focus on the problems of the world creates people who feel discontent, and who then choose fictive contentment over their freedoms. This system enables exploitation and creates one of the world's biggest problems: contentment can be, and is, misused to manipulate and thereby control others. The discontentment that occurred on Black Thursday, October 1929, when the Wall Street Stock Market crashed, resulted in the Great Depression. The psychopathic collectivist dictator Adolf Hitler perfectly utilized the economic catastrophe in Germany to rise to power, causing World War II. Eventually, 6 million Jews were killed in the name of national-socialism, and the total casualties of World War II are estimated to have reached 60 million. Conversely, to avoid similar events from happening again, the search for security opened new doors and led to the creation of the European Union—relying on socialism and big governments once again, the exact same source of authoritarian collectivist control that caused the devastation in the first place. And so the source that promised to guarantee our liberty moved from one occupational force, the national socialists, to Marxism's latest passive-aggressive approach, which is the occupational force controlled emotionally by narcissists, the nationalistic democratic socialists. A movement that has been furthered by the general worldwide misperception that Hitler's national-socialism was the act of the right wing.

The exact same resentment and anger also drove the socialist activist (the perceived collectivist hero) Che Guevara on his killing spree across the South American continent, in Cuba, and in Africa; Guevara's estimated personal body count totaled 4,000. The ruthless psychopathic dictators Joseph Stalin, allegedly responsible for as many as 40 million deaths, and Mao Zedong, allegedly responsible for well over 70 million deaths, are both examples of Marxist dictators. Both men, though socialists / communists who rose to power by advancing social equality, lived like kings in luxury palaces while their subservient citizens lived, and still live, impoverished lives.

Since 9/11, insecurity has effectively empowered governments worldwide while revoking their citizen's freedoms by the minute. Delivered to the populace as necessary security, the domestic tyranny daily grows more and more obvious. All this has been achieved through camouflage by the perfect diversion: discontentment through the fear of terrorism, climate change, and the current Great Recession. Thus, our biggest threat is our supposed protectors, the governments themselves.

Most questionable will be the outcome of severe inflation potentially occurring in the United States in the near future. Should this happen, when the government is unable to print money out if thin air to make up for the United States debt, assuredly the outcome will be an even greater depression leading to dependency in the American populace. America, a great nation built on independence, will then be a dependent nation. Likely, once again, this will cause its populace to turn to government for support (the same source that caused the problem in the first place), similar to what took place in post-WWII Europe, that being dependency leading to a strong support of totalitarian-collectivism.

A question that always comes to mind is why the money should be funneled through the state. If the government wants to compel its citizens to take care of others, then why doesn't it impose laws on its people to donate a percentage of their earnings to charities and those in need? Thus, this question is answered quite thoroughly in this exposé. The power of authority invested in one single organism with access to blackmail and bribery, combined with every possible means of coercion available to enforce this extortion (military, police, and justice) dooms the people for tyranny, death, and destruction.

The exact reason being that totalitarian-collectivist ideals are built on bad boundaries, the inability, or unwillingness, to recognize boundaries between self and society, because collectivists feel (1) a strong sense of entitlement, hence, they fail to identify with the feelings of others (rights to personal choice, privacy, preferences, and priorities) caused by (2) lack of empathy, which comes as a consequence of extreme inferiority complex, and the resultant (3) grandiose sense of self-importance, perfectly assessed by collectivist ideals—the notion of social equality—allowing sensations of moral superiority a true source of attention, affirmation, adulation, narcissistic supply, their (4) required excessive admiration attained through (5) preoccupation with success (fantasies of the perfect utopian society without any poverty, where all people have equal opportunities and are treated entirely equal); again leading them to believe that the populace should be rewarded without mandatory achievement, which is perfect justification for being (6) envious of people of a better standing whom they believe should share their private assets, and consequently, because they (7) consider themselves special and by means of excessive self-righteousness using projections to dump shame on others, as well as (8) arrogance (magical thinking) to debase anyone opposing truth, and allowing the collectivist to create the perfect pathological illusion and thereby to (9) exploit society for personal gain.

Throughout history, tampering with nature's ways has proven unforeseeable and often with devastating consequences. In this case, the naturally occurring societal class-differences that enables incentive to create necessary self-esteem (e.g., psychological resilience) are destroyed, therefore, social equality causes severe inferiority complex and hence psychopathic mental illness. To this day, no philosophy or religion comes even near the genocide, tyranny, and damage that the theories of Marxism (big governments) have caused to mankind, with death tolls estimated to be near 100 million. The genocide on individualism continues.

Solution Thoughts

- No war has ever been fought without being subject to narcissism, either caused by grandiose sensations (feelings of being more right than others and hunger for power or exploitation for personal gain). If there is a purpose to life it is undoubtedly to fight this evil, which can be accomplished in one way only, simply by bettering ourselves—to fight narcissism from within.
- Narcissism (inferiority complex) causes adolescent bullying in the school system. Striking down on the problem would be a powerful tool. The magnitude and importance of addressing the source that facilitates collectivism in its early stages would truly advance society—through cognitive study of self and through subjective teachings of psychology (psychopathy and narcissism) and other personality disorders as a mandatory part the curriculum.

- Breakthroughs and progress can come through tools available through psychology and use of therapy. In this manner, it is possible to accomplish the significance of embracing the confident mentality: to encourage benign envy, self-assurance, and self-encouragement, to oppose unhealthy narcissism, to combat those who denigrate others for expressing their self-assuredness, as well as to heal, strengthen, and uphold higher subconscious awareness.
- In politics, the narcissist and psychopath has the absolute advantage, however, only until exposed. Recruiting psychological advisers specialized in psychopathic mental disorders would, therefore, put that advantage back in the right hands.

In today's Western nations, opportunities are plentiful and subordinated only by bureaucratic involvement. Our current situations are quite unlike the way society looked in the eighteenth century, when Marxism began to emerge. Unlike third-world societies, where life is truly difficult, a person in today's Western world who has no disabilities has no legitimate excuse for not being able to make it given the numerous options available. Why should helping anyone in the Western world in any way be different than the way we aid people in third-world countries: help to self-help. And just like in third-world countries, why do we not safeguard that investment by means of following the investment and assuring progression and succession—the goal of self-sustainability. Everyone is, and should be, one's own master of happiness. Equality is never achieved by evading personal responsibility, but earned only through pain, sacrifice, and hardship by claiming personal responsibility.

With these words, you may ask, "Do I believe I am more right than any collectivist?" The answer I would give is, "No, not necessarily." Freedom gives anyone the right to their ideals, but as well, freedom takes away one's right to force one's ideals upon others. Freedom does have consequences, as well as casualties that should be addressed; thus, the consequences and casualties of freedom are by far less than the outcome of losing freedom itself.

> *"Insanity: doing the same thing over and over again and expecting different results."*
> *—ALBERT EINSTEIN*

A Token of My Appreciation

Research, writing, and promotion is costly and time-consuming, and so I wish to declare my most sincere gratitude to you for purchasing this book.

Revenue generated from this purchase helps continue my research and in reaching a wider audience and maximizing public exposure. Without your contribution, liberty cannot succeed.

OTHER CDES PUBLISHING BOOKS YOU MAY ENJOY

Normal Coffee at the Head Wound Café

By Dennis Paul Lutz

(Available on Amazon, Kindle, the author's website, cdespublishing.com, and other retail book outlets)

Normal Coffee at the Head Wound Café is a tale from the eerie space of psychological fiction, where the aberrant or damaged brain must try to make sense of the world as it is dimly being perceived. DePaul Lewitz mumbles through his day at the sanitarium, reviewing randomly selected events of his family history and the happenings in his surroundings with certain assurance of an irrational rendering.

The second feature is the story of "The Place Where Dreams Go to Die" explores the life of Robert Angelloti – son of "Fat Gino", alleged to be a noted Philadelphia crime boss as Robert seeks to discover what 'important' thing he was born to accomplish.

Finally we have the short story – The Rapture, a short story, sneak peek into Dennis Paul Lutz's next foray into authorship – a collection of short stories - Tales from the Airstream

OTHER CDES PUBLISHING BOOKS YOU MAY ENJOY

Raventross

By John Burwell Wilkes

(Available on Amazon, Kindle, the author's websites, cdespublishing.com, and other retail book outlets)

The Cabal of Clairvaux Series – Book One

The first book in The Cabal of Clairvaux Series, Raventross is an aviation adventure, full of flying action, thrills, suspense, mystery, and even a love story. The plot evolves around a highly classified very black project which is often sinister with huge implications and dangers for the entire planet.

Although this amazing story could never have been told until now, it has been acclaimed by critics to have the excitement of Star Chamber, Foxfire, and Top Gun all rolled into one. The characters, the times, and the places are real. The intentions, the risks, and the stakes, are high. Raventross definitely "pushes the envelope."

ABOUT CDES PUBLISHING LLC

CDES Publishing LLC is an independent book publisher and a member of the Independent Book Publishers' Association. In today's rapidly changing book marketplace, we have adapted and developed a somewhat unique 'middle ground' paradigm between the traditional publishers who, from an author's point of view, are virtually inapproachable without having 'A-List' literary agency representation, and the vanity press outfits who are mostly 'print shops' for hire masquerading as publishers.

We enter into co-publishing contracts with authors whose work we believe merits publication. We split the costs of publication and promotion with the author and we split the revenue generated. If the book doesn't sell, the author has saved enough to try a couple more times, compared to the expense of a traditional vanity press self-publishing option. If the book sells modestly well – the author may earn 3 or 4 times as much as he would have, working under a standard new author contract with a traditional publisher.

If self-publishing is what you want to do – but you have certain 'holes' in your skill set, for example, interior layout, cover design, press releases, registering copyright, obtaining an LCCN, an ISBN, an EAN compliant barcode, arranging for reviews, setting up a website to promote your book, creating an eBook edition of your work – give us a call. We can also provide these services on an a la carte basis.

CDES Publishing LLC 1101 E Tropicana Ave PMB 2166 Las Vegas, NV 89119-6629	(702) 560-1853 sales@cdespublishing.com http://www.cdespublishing.com

Made in the USA
San Bernardino, CA
07 May 2015